Why the
BIBLE
Makes
Sense

As History, As Ultimate Truth, As Guide for Life

BARBOUR
PUBLISHING

© 2013 by Barbour Publishing, Inc.

Print ISBN 978-1-62029-863-3

eBook Editions:
Adobe Digital Edition (.epub) 978-1-62416-407-1
Kindle and MobiPocket Edition (.prc) 978-1-62416-406-4

Cover image © Paul Calbar, istockphoto.com

Published by Barbour Publishing, Inc., P.O. Box 719, Uhrichsville, Ohio 44683, www.barbourbooks.com

Our mission is to publish and distribute inspirational products offering exceptional value and biblical encouragement to the masses.

Member of the
Evangelical Christian
Publishers Association

Printed in the United States of America.

Contents

Why Obeying God Makes Sense

Is the Bible Still Relevant Today?

Understanding the Bible

Making Sense of a Suffering World

Introduction

The Bible makes sense on so many levels. The historical events it describes line up with other solid historical sources, and archaeological discoveries—including some very recent ones—continually confirm the accuracy of the scriptures. The Bible also makes sense as ultimate truth; what it says about the beginning of the universe and humankind is rational—the opinions of critical scientists notwithstanding. And finally, the Bible's moral truths, from the Ten Commandments to the teachings of Jesus, make excellent sense as a guide for life.

Christians believe that the Bible is true, but there's more to it than that. The apostle Paul declared that our faith is both "true and reasonable" (Acts 26:25 NIV). However, if you don't know your Bible well or haven't thought through the reasons behind its truths, when family members, friends, or acquaintances ask questions, you may not be able to adequately "give. . .a reason for the hope that is in you" (1 Peter 3:15 NKJV).

In addition, with just a few clicks on the Internet, critics can find articles that contend that the Bible is unreliable or full of contradictions—or argue that all the suffering in the world is proof that God doesn't exist—or that the Bible is outdated and no longer relevant today. *Why the Bible Makes Sense* will help you respond to such assertions. While this book isn't an exhaustive resource, we hope it will help you explain the basic reasons why the Bible makes sense.

For this reason, it also discusses the creation of the Old and New Testaments, and the copying of their text. Does it make a difference to know that the Bible is truly God's inspired Word, and that the scripture text we have today is trustworthy? You bet it does! *Why the Bible Makes Sense* also examines some difficult textual questions and supposed contradictions.

If you are skeptical or have doubts about any of the Bible's statements, we trust that this book will begin to answer your questions and show you that Christian faith is not only true but also reasonable. It makes good sense.

ArchaeoLogic: Throughout this book, you'll find brief notes that show how archaelogical discoveries directly support statements made in God's Word. That's ArchaeoLogic!

The Writing of the Old Testament

1. Moses Wrote the Law

Moses wrote the Law (the Torah) personally, since he was highly educated and literate (see Acts 7:22). Writing was prevalent at that time, about 1445 BC. Not only were hieroglyphics and cursive hieratic script used in Egypt, but Akkadian cuneiform was also used for diplomatic correspondence between Canaan and Egypt. Furthermore, the Sinaitic alphabet was used widely throughout the Sinai, Canaan, and Phoenicia.

Moses was a real, historical person, and the Torah repeatedly states that he wrote the Law as God gave it: "And Moses wrote all the words of the LORD" (Exodus 24:4 NKJV). "So Moses wrote this law and delivered it to the priests, the sons of Levi" (Deuteronomy 31:9 NKJV; see also Exodus 17:14; Numbers 33:2; Deuteronomy 31:22, 24).

However, in 1876–1877, Julius Wellhausen argued that the Law was fabricated in Moses' name. This documentary hypothesis is also called JEDP, because it contends that the Torah was created from the following: (J) the Jehovah/Yahweh source, written about 950 BC; (E) the Elohim/El source, written about 850 BC; (D) the Deuteronomic source, written about 600 BC; (P) the Priestly source, written about 500 BC. Finally, editors supposedly combined all the sources, creating the Torah in its present form around 450 BC.

In 1987, however, R. N. Whybray pointed out JEDP's logical fallacies, asking, if the Yahweh and Elohim sources had scrupulously avoided duplication and contradictory themes, why did editors (trying to create a believable "pious fraud") combine them? Since 1987, Wellhausen's hypothesis has been replaced by many conflicting, sometimes radically different, theories.

Paul warned: "For a time is coming when people . . .will look for teachers who will tell them whatever their itching ears want to hear. They will reject the truth and chase after myths" (2 Timothy 4:3–4 NLT).

ArchaeoLogic: The Amarna letters are 382 tablets discovered in Akhetaten (the ancient capital of Egypt) in 1887 and were written when the Hebrews were still conquering Canaan (Judges 1); many of the tablets contain pleas from Canaanite kings for help against the attacking *Habiru*.

---

2. The Writing of Genesis

Many people have this question niggling in the back of their minds: "But what about Genesis? It was written before Moses' day." Yes, it was, with the emphasis on "written." Skeptics have long insisted that the accounts of Abraham, Isaac, and Jacob existed as oral traditions for hundreds of years. Therefore, the argument goes, the stories—while being passed down by word of mouth—became so garbled that they have little or no actual historical value.

However, Genesis 11:27–28 says that Abraham (about 2166–1991 BC) emigrated from Ur, and writing (even schools) existed there. Abraham was a wealthy man and was either literate or had a scribe in his employ. In addition, thousands of clay tablets containing writing in phonetic Semitic cuneiform have been discovered at the ancient city of Ebla, two hundred miles north of Canaan; many of these writings date to 2500 BC, before Abraham was even born.

In addition, the book of Genesis has indications of being written in stages as each generation added their story to the narrative. For example, Genesis 35:27–29 describes Jacob returning to his father, and Isaac's death a few years after. The story of Jacob's life and adventures was written by then. Before Isaac died, however, Jacob's son Joseph had been presumed dead. But after Jacob learned that Joseph was still alive, Joseph's story begins (in the period *before* Isaac's death).

Moreover, the cultural elements mentioned in Genesis, from traditions to laws to styles of covenants, all bear the earmarks of authenticity for the time and area that they were said to have happened in. In other words, they are accurate historical accounts.

3. The Honest, Accurate Chroniclers

Few people in the ancient Near East could read and write since formal education was a luxury not many could afford. Those who did receive such training were in demand as scribes. Scribes not only meticulously copied out the scriptures but also kept track of inventory and served as royal secretaries who handled correspondence and recorded the daily events of a king's reign. For example, David's uncle Jehonathan was his counselor and scribe (1 Chronicles 27:32).

Scribes also composed chronicles of the history of the kings. In Egypt, Assyria, and other kingdoms scribes often wrote exaggerated reports of kings' victories and downplayed or omitted their failures. In sharp contrast, the writers of the Bible's historical books honestly preserved the nation's often-unflattering history. David's sins concerning Bathsheba and the dismal failures of many other kings are all on record.

The reason for this exceptional level of truthfulness is that the men who wrote Israel's history were often the *same* individuals who had fearlessly rebuked the kings when they sinned. The prophets Samuel, Nathan, and Gad recorded the events of David's reign (see 1 Samuel 10:25; 1 Chronicles 29:29–30). The prophet Shemaiah wrote the chronicles of King Rehoboam's reign (see 1 Kings 12:22–44; 2 Chronicles 12:5–8, 15). And the prophet Jehu wrote King Jehoshaphat's biography (see 2 Chronicles 19:2; 20:34), just to name a few.

As for accuracy, these prophets were there when the events they described happened. The godly men who later compiled the books of 1 and 2 Kings and 1 and 2 Chronicles had access to the original royal documents (see 1 Kings 15:7, 23, 31; 16:5, 14, 20, 27; etc.).

ArchaeoLogic: Khirbet Qeiyafa (biblical Shaaraim) dates to the time of Saul (1 Samuel 17:52), and the Qeiyafa Ostracon, discovered there in 2008, is a pottery shard containing five lines of text. According to epigrapher Emile Puech, it describes Saul being chosen as Israel's first king.

---

4. Professional Scribes and Secretaries

Not all prophets of God were literate. God sometimes chose men and women of humble backgrounds to speak His word (Amos 7:14–15). Even though the prophet Jeremiah could read and write (Jeremiah 51:60), he often depended on Baruch, a professional scribe from a leading family, who was trained to take dictation:

"Then Jeremiah called Baruch. . .and Baruch wrote on a scroll of a book, at the instruction of Jeremiah, the words of the LORD which He had spoken to him." When asked about the process, Baruch explained, "He proclaimed with his mouth all these words to me, and I wrote them with ink in the book" (Jeremiah 36:4, 18 NKJV).

Until the exile to Babylon, most scribes didn't copy out scriptures. Rather, most were either government secretaries or ordinary public scribes who could be hired to write down legal documents, take letters by dictation, and keep accountant's records. The priests had their own highly literate members who copied out scriptures. Only after the return from Babylon did the term *scribe* refer specifically to those who copied and preserved the scriptures.

Because they slowly, painstakingly, carefully copied out each word letter by letter, the scribes became intimately familiar with the tiniest shades of meaning of God's Word—so it was natural that by Jesus' day they would rise to prominence as "experts of the Law" and interpreters of its meaning.

5. Copying the Scriptures

At first only the temple and the royal palace had copies of the scriptures (Deuteronomy 17:18), and when those were misplaced, it was a near disaster (1 Kings 22:3–10). But after the temple was destroyed in 586 BC and the Jews went into exile in Babylon, there was a major change. Synagogues arose, places where Jews met to pray and hear God's Word being read.

When the Jews returned to Israel seventy years later, they began building synagogues in all their towns, and every synagogue had a copy of the scriptures. The book of 1 Maccabees, though not part of the Bible, is considered a reliable historical source, and describes this practice in 1 Maccabees 1:56–58. (See also Acts 15:21.)

Back in Babylon, a special class of scribes had arisen to make copies of the scriptures. Ezra, the leading scribe during the return from exile, is believed to be the founding father of this movement (Ezra 7:6, 10). The scribes who followed Ezra took great pains to ensure that they made accurate copies. Nevertheless, a few minor errors crept into the texts from time to time, although these didn't usually change the meaning in any significant way.

During the AD 600s to 900s Jewish scribes called Masoretes enforced very strict rules for making copies of the text and added helpful vowel points to the consonants. This reduced scribal errors dramatically. The Masoretic text was so renowned for being error-free that it was accepted as the official version of the Old Testament. But you may ask: What about inaccuracies introduced into the text *before* the Masoretes?

ArchaeoLogic: The Bible describes how around 840 BC, Mesha king of Moab (a vassal of Israel) rebelled against the king of Israel after Ahab died. In 1868, the Mesha Stele was found in Jordan. It is Mesha's own account of his rebellion, dedicated to his god, Chemosh.

6. The Dead Sea Scrolls

Until 1947, skeptics argued that there were likely so many mistakes in the Hebrew text that there was no way of telling *how* closely the Masoretic text (MT) resembled the original documents. That year, however, a remarkable discovery was made. Jars full of ancient scrolls were found in caves near the Dead Sea in Israel; these scrolls—copied by the Qumran community—dated back nearly two thousand years to 150 BC–AD 70, with a few from 250 BC. There are at least fragments of every Old Testament book except for Esther.

The Dead Sea Scrolls have confirmed the remarkable accuracy of the MT. It was found to be virtually identical to a large segment of the ancient copies. For example:

The prophet Isaiah lived until about 680 BC, but before the Dead Sea Scrolls were found, the earliest copy of Isaiah was an MT scroll from about AD 980, some fifteen hundred years later. The Isaiah scroll found at Qumran was copied between 150 and 100 BC. Scholars were astonished at how closely our modern text agreed with it. More than 95 percent of the text was identical, and the 5 percent differences were mostly different spellings of a word and obvious slips of the pen.

Isaiah is filled with Messianic prophecies, and it's important to be certain that the text we have today says the same things as the original text by Isaiah—and it does! For example, Isaiah 53, remarkably fulfilled by Jesus, contains a few stylistic changes and spelling mistakes in the Dead Sea Scrolls, and three letters (for the word *light*) were added in verse 11, but other than that, this powerful prophecy is identical.

7. The "Daniel Fraud" Debunked

The book of Daniel claims to have been composed by the prophet himself (Daniel 9:2; 10:2), with its final chapter written around 530 BC. However, because it contains prophecies of future events—many of which were fulfilled in following centuries—skeptics argue that Daniel is a "pious fraud" actually written 200–160 BC, *after* the events had taken place. Many theorize it was written during the persecution of Antiochus Epiphanes (165 BC) to encourage the Jews.

The evidence in the Dead Sea Scrolls, however, argues strongly that the book of Daniel is authentic and was written centuries earlier. For one thing, the Qumran community composed their own doctrinal writings during this same period (200–100 BC), yet the Hebrew and Aramaic in the book of Daniel are noticeably more archaic. Furthermore, the Aramaic Daniel used was an eastern dialect used in Babylon, not the western dialect spoken in Israel.

Critics point to the presence of three Greek loanwords in Daniel 3, insisting that they prove that Daniel was written after Alexander conquered Israel in 332 BC. But Greek mercenaries and traders had traveled the world for centuries before Alexander's conquest.

Eight copies of the book of Daniel have been found at Qumran (all of which agree closely with the MT text), and in their writings the Qumran community refers to Daniel the same way they refer to canonical scripture, saying: "which was written in the book of Daniel the prophet." One fragment of a Daniel scroll dates to 125 BC, only a few years after critics say the book was composed—yet it was *already* considered scripture *and* was written in a different Aramaic *and* in archaic Hebrew that was no longer used.

Fulfilled Bible Prophecy

8. The Fall of an Oppressor

Many people are willing to concede that the Bible contains an accurate record of Israel's history. But they're not ready to admit that the miracles it describes *also* happened or that the Bible is the very word of God—or that God actually exists. Fulfilled prophecy, however, is definitive proof of the Bible's divine inspiration.

Around 630 BC, when the prophet Nahum described the soon-coming doom of Nineveh, capital of the Assyrian Empire, it didn't seem likely. The Assyrians were an oppressive warrior-state with a powerful military; they were unspeakably cruel to the nations they conquered—and they were at the very height of their power. Great Nineveh itself was protected by five walls, with the inner wall one hundred feet high and four chariot-widths thick. And since Nineveh was at the junction of two rivers, it was guarded on several sides by water.

Nevertheless, Nahum prophesied that Nineveh would be besieged and conquered (Nahum 2:1–4; 3:1–3, 14–15). And he predicted exactly how the city would fall: "But with an overflowing flood He will make an utter end of its place. . . . The gates of the rivers are opened" (Nahum 1:8; 2:6 NKJV).

Less than twenty years later, armies of Babylonians and Medes surrounded Nineveh. After two years of siege, the attackers built a dam on the Khoser River (which ran through the city). Then, in 612 BC, they opened the river gates and the resulting flood washed away part of the city's wall, allowing them to enter. So complete was Nineveh's destruction that when Alexander the Great fought a battle nearby in 331 BC, he saw no evidence that a city had ever been there.

ArchaeoLogic: There used to be no evidence of the ancient Assyrian city of Nineveh, so skeptics said that the Bible was just making it up. Then, in 1842, its ancient city mound was discovered. Today, the city of Nineveh has been extensively excavated.

9. Naming an Unborn King, Cyrus

Around 680 BC Isaiah prophesied: "Thus says the LORD to His anointed, to Cyrus, whose right hand I have held—to subdue nations before him...that you may know that I, the LORD, who call you by your name, am the God of Israel" (Isaiah 45:1, 3 NKJV). "I have raised him up. . .he shall build my city, and he shall let go my captives" (Isaiah 45:13 KJV). "I am the LORD. . .who says of Cyrus, 'He is My shepherd, and he shall perform all My pleasure, saying to Jerusalem, "You shall be built," and to the temple, "Your foundation shall be laid"'" (Isaiah 44:24, 28 NKJV).

At the time of this prophecy Jerusalem was still intact, the temple was still standing, and the people of Judea hadn't gone into captivity (exile). All that changed in 586 BC when the Babylonians sacked the city, burned the temple, and took the Jews to Babylon.

Who was Cyrus? Well, twenty years after Isaiah's prophecy, Cyrus I reigned in Anshan in Persia from 600 BC to 580 BC. But that wasn't the Cyrus mentioned in Isaiah 45. His son Cambyses I reigned from 580BC to 559 BC, under the kings of Media. His son, Cyrus II, reigned 559–530 BC, and in 549 BC he defeated the Medes and went on to conquer their empire—and to fulfill Isaiah's prophecies.

In 538 BC Cyrus issued his Edict of Restoration, allowing all exiled peoples, including the Jews, to return to their homelands. He let the Jews rebuild Jerusalem, and declared: "This is what Cyrus king of Persia says: 'The LORD, the God of heaven, has given me all the kingdoms of the earth and he has appointed me to build a temple for him at Jerusalem'" (Ezra 1:2 NIV).

10. The Rise and Fall of Two Empires

The book of Daniel contains very specific prophecies about future kingdoms. The rise and fall of two empires is one of the most spectacular. Around 551 BC, God gave Daniel a vision of a powerful two-horned ram that vanquished every opponent. Then a goat with one prominent horn between his eyes came from the west and charged the ram, shattering his horns and trampling the ram underfoot. But at the height of his power, the goat's large horn was broken off and four horns grew up in its place (Daniel 8:1–8).

Daniel was told that the two-horned ram represented the kings of Media and Persia, the goat was the king of Greece, and the large horn was its first great king. The four horns were four kingdoms that would emerge from his nation (Daniel 8:20–22).

Sure enough, in 539 BC, the Medo-Persian army conquered Babylon, bringing the Babylonian Empire to an end. The Medo-Persian Empire then ruled the world until 334 BC. At that time, Alexander the Great swept out of Greece (the west) and defeated the Persian army in a series of battles between 334 and 330 BC. He then went on to conquer much of the rest of the world. At the height of his power, in 323 BC, Alexander died, after which his four generals divided his empire into four smaller empires.

According to Josephus (*Antiquities* XI, viii, 5), when Alexander conquered cities on his way south to Egypt, the Jews opened the gates of Jerusalem. After they showed him Daniel's prophecies about him conquering the Persians, Alexander spared Israel.

> **ArchaeoLogic:** Ben-Hadad, king of Aram, was waging a losing war with Assyria, but Hazael killed Ben-Hadad and ruled (2 Kings 8:7–15). An inscription by Shalmaneser of Assyria says, "I fought with Ben-Hadad. I accomplished his defeat. Hazael, son of a nobody, seized his throne."

11. Jesus and the Jewish Revolt

In AD 30, Jesus prophesied that Jerusalem would be besieged by armies, and the people within her would be killed: "The days will come upon you when your enemies will build an embankment against you and encircle you and hem you in on every side. They will dash you to the ground, you and the children within your walls. . .because you did not recognize the time of God's coming to you" (Luke 19:43–44 NIV).

In AD 66 the Jews revolted against Rome, but the Romans struck back, retook the country, and were soon besieging Jerusalem itself. They dug a trench around the city and built a high wall around that, just as Jesus had warned. The Jewish historian Josephus, in *The Wars of the Jews*, described the capture of the city in AD 70, and the slaughter that followed.

Jesus had also prophesied: "They will be killed by the sword or sent away as captives to all the nations of the world" (Luke 21:24 NLT). Josephus claimed that 1,100,000 Jews were killed during the siege and 97,000 were sold as slaves throughout the Roman Empire. Some 6,000 prisoners of war ended up in Greece cutting the Corinth Canal.

Jesus predicted that the Jewish temple would be utterly destroyed: "Assuredly, I say to you, not one stone shall be left here upon another, that shall not be thrown down" (Matthew 24:2 NKJV). And it was. The cedar paneling inside the temple was set on fire, and the intense heat melted all the gold covering the temple. The Roman soldiers then took apart the temple stone by stone to get at the gold.

12. The Suffering Messiah

King David lived almost a thousand years before Jesus died on the cross and before the Romans conquered Israel and practiced crucifixion there—yet in Psalm 22 (NIV) David gave a chilling description of crucifixion.

"They pierce my hands and my feet" (v. 16). In crucifixion, nails were driven through the hands and feet of the condemned man. "All my bones are out of joint" (v. 14). A person's arms were often pulled from their sockets while hanging on a cross. "All my bones are on display" (v. 17). The Romans routinely whipped condemned men before crucifying them; their muscles were cut open so badly that their bones were visible. "I am poured out like water" (v. 14). Blood poured freely out of the many lacerations, resulting in severe blood loss.

"My mouth is dried up" (v. 15). One of the side effects of crucifixion is dehydration; this is the reason Jesus said, "I am thirsty" (John 19:28 NIV). "People stare and gloat over me" (v. 17). Jesus was executed publicly, and many people stared at him as they passed by; His enemies openly mocked Him (Matthew 27:41–43). "They divide my clothes among them and cast lots for my garment" (v. 18). The Roman guards did indeed divide His clothing and rolled dice to see who would get His robe (John 19:23–24).

How could David describe Christ's death with such accuracy? He could do so because "prophecy never came by the will of man, but holy men of God spoke as they were moved by the Holy Spirit" (2 Peter 1:21 NKJV).

ArchaeoLogic: The Black Obelisk, found in the palace of Shalmaneser of Assyria, states: "The tribute of Iaua mar Hu-umrii [Jehu son of Omri]: I have received. . . ." Jehoram was grandson of Omri, but Jehu slew Jehoram and took his place as king of Israel (2 Kings 9).

13. Astonishing Messianic Prophecies

The prevalent view of the Jews in Jesus' day was that their Messiah would come as a conquering king, drive out the Romans, and immediately set up the kingdom of God in Israel. Yet Isaiah 53 (NIV) describes a suffering servant of God.

"He was oppressed and afflicted, yet he did not open his mouth" (v. 7). Jesus amazed the chief priest, Pilate, and Herod by staying silent and not answering their questions (Matthew 27:12–14; Mark 14:60–61; Luke 23:8–9).

Isaiah states that "he was led like a lamb to the slaughter" (v. 7). Jesus was crucified on Passover when the Passover lambs were killed, and John the Baptist had called Him the "Lamb of God" who takes away the sin of the world (John 1:29).

"But he was pierced for our transgressions" (v. 5). Jesus' hands and feet were pierced when the Roman soldiers nailed Him to the cross.

Isaiah prophesied that "he had done no violence, nor was any deceit in his mouth" (v. 9), yet He "was numbered with the transgressors" (v. 12). Jesus quoted this last passage in Luke 22:37, saying that He was about to fulfill it. Although He hadn't committed a violent crime, He was crucified with two criminals who had (Luke 23:32, 39–41).

"He was assigned a grave with the wicked, and with the rich in his death" (v. 9). Jesus would've been buried in a graveyard for executed criminals, but at the last minute, a wealthy man, Joseph of Arimathea, received permission to bury Jesus in his own tomb (Matthew 27:57–60).

14. The Resurrected Son of God

One of the most solidly attested truths of the Gospel is that on the third day after Jesus died on the cross and was laid in a tomb, God raised Him from the dead, never to die again. Jesus' resurrection fulfilled this thousand-year-old prophecy by David:

"No wonder my heart is glad, and I rejoice. My body rests in safety. For you will not leave my soul among the dead or allow your holy one to rot in the grave. You will show me the way of life, granting me the joy of your presence and the pleasures of living with you forever" (Psalm 16:9–11 NLT).

The apostles Peter and Paul proclaimed that Jesus had fulfilled this prophecy (see Acts 2:24–32; 13:35–37). Peter stated, "You can be sure that the patriarch David wasn't referring to himself, for he died and was buried, and his tomb is still here among us. . . . David was looking into the future and speaking of the Messiah's resurrection" (Acts 2:29, 31 NLT).

Jesus Himself had repeatedly prophesied that He would be arrested, mocked, beaten, and killed—but that on the third day He would be resurrected from the dead. He first told His disciples about this almost one year before it happened, and in the following months He repeated this prediction (see Matthew 16:21; 17:22–23; 20:18–19).

And what does Jesus' resurrection prove? It proves that He is the one and only Son of God. As

Paul stated, Jesus Christ was "declared to be the Son of God with power according to the Spirit of holiness, by the resurrection from the dead" (Romans 1:4 NKJV).

> **ArchaeoLogic:** The Nazareth Decree, a slab of marble acquired from Nazareth around 1878, was a ruling by Caesar forbidding the disturbing of tombs, extracting the buried and transferring them to other places. This was quite likely written in response to the rumors of Matthew 28:11–15.

The Writing of the New Testament

15. Synoptic Gospels and Pericopes

Those who read the Gospels are struck by the similarity between the first three—Matthew, Mark, and Luke. Although they each contain unique material, they repeat most of the same stories and incidents, usually in the same order. When you study them in detail, the similarities are even more remarkable. Often when the Gospels relate the same incident or saying, they repeat it almost word for word—sometimes *exactly* word for word. (Compare Matthew 3:7–10 and Luke 3:7–9.)

This is why Matthew, Mark, and Luke are called the synoptic Gospels: *synoptic* means "seen together," because they contain parallel texts.

The many short, self-contained stories are called *pericopes*, a Greek word that means "a cutting out." It appears that these stories were written down and compiled early on, and that the Gospel writers then used these existing pericopes—generally following the same timeline, but sometimes re-arranging and/or editing the material slightly to suit their intended audience. This is what happened, but God directly guided the process.

The Gospel of John, however, is noticeably different. For the most part, John completely skips retelling the already-known pericopes about Jesus, and focuses on new material. Fully 90 percent of John's account consists of material not found in the other Gospels. And it's a good thing: otherwise, we'd have missed many of the unique stories that his Gospel preserves.

16. The Earliest Written Gospel

You commonly hear scholars state that Mark was the first Gospel committed to writing, and that Matthew and Luke based their Gospels on Mark's text and added extra material from other sources. This is close to the truth but not entirely accurate since Mark's Gospel contains numerous small, vivid additions that don't appear in the parallel texts in Matthew and Luke.

Mark is the shortest Gospel, containing the story of Jesus with almost none of the parables or stories found in Matthew and Luke. Mark is only 661 verses long, yet 606 of those verses (often quoted word for word) are found in Matthew. Fully 92 percent of Mark appears in Matthew. And 350 verses from Mark appear with little change in Luke. But this isn't proof that the writers of the other two synoptic Gospels copied Mark.

Rather, it's more likely that Jesus' apostles wrote the original, official account of His words and deeds early on, before AD 50, in a *protoevangelium* ("first gospel"). They had, after all, been specifically commissioned by Jesus to preach the Gospel and were devoted "continually to. . .the ministry of the word" (Acts 6:2, 4 NKJV). Then Mark, Matthew, and Luke all based their Gospels on *this* document.

Church tradition tells us that Mark produced his Gospel under the guidance of the apostle Peter, to whom he was like a son (1 Peter 5:13). Mark added the least material, mostly enlivening the existing text with brief notes from Peter. Scholars note that Mark's additions sound very much like vivid eyewitness details.

For their parts, Matthew and Luke added numerous (and sometimes lengthy) stories, sayings, and parables from "sayings" sources.

> **ArchaeoLogic:** Archaeologists have discovered the highly fortified, twin-towered temple of Baal-berith in Shechem mentioned in Judges 9:4. Abimelech, king of Shechem, destroyed the temple and its towers (Judges 9:46–49) during the twelfth century BC.

17. Early Written "Sayings" Sources

Contrary to what you might have heard, Jesus' teachings didn't exist as half-memorized oral stories for forty years until they were finally written down in the Gospels after 70 AD. They probably existed in written form from the earliest days.

In the Roman world, even highly literate people dictated letters. The prolific Roman orator/statesman Cicero (106–43 BC) is a good example of this. Cicero's slave, Tiro, not only wrote letters by dictation but also is believed to have been the one who collected and published all of Cicero's now-famous writings after his death.

One hundred years after Cicero, Jesus' apostles used scribes also. When Paul wanted to write an important message in AD 57, he dictated it to a companion who added at the end, "I, Tertius, the one writing this letter for Paul, send my greetings, too" (Romans 16:22 NLT). Peter also wrote a letter with the help of Silas (1 Peter 5:12).

Since people before *and* after Jesus employed scribes to preserve their thoughts in writing, why would Jesus leave it to chance that His disciples would remember His vitally important teachings forty years after He spoke them? Think about it: Matthew quoted lengthy chunks of Jesus' sayings in chapters 5, 6, and 7, and John (sixty years after AD 30) quoted Jesus verbatim in chapters 14, 15, 16, and 17. These words had to have been written down early.

Of all Jesus' disciples, Matthew was most likely the scribe, since he'd been a tax collector, a job that required him to be fluent in both Greek and Aramaic, and to quickly write accurate, detailed records.

18. When the Gospels Were Written

Many scholars argue that the Gospels were written after AD 70. The Romans destroyed the Jewish temple that year, as Jesus had prophesied (Mark 13:1–2; Matthew 24:1–2; Luke 21:20–24). But skeptics say that the Gospels were composed late and this "prophecy" placed in Jesus' mouth *after* the fact.

However, the historian Eusebius (in *Ecclesiastical History*, bk. 3, ch. 24) states that Matthew wrote his Gospel just before leaving Israel for distant lands. The apostles were still in Jerusalem in AD 49/50 because Paul met the "apostles and elders" there then (Acts 15:2, 4, 6). However, when Paul went to Jerusalem in AD 57, he met "James, and all the elders" (Acts 21:17–18 NIV), but no apostles. They were gone. So Matthew composed his Gospel between AD 50 and 56.

Luke's Gospel and the book of Acts are two parts of one work (Luke 1:3; Acts 1:1). Luke wrote Acts about AD 61, because Paul was released from his first imprisonment in AD 62, yet Acts ends with him still under house arrest (Acts 28:30–31). In Acts, Luke refers to his "former book" (Acts 1:1 NIV), so he wrote his Gospel no later than AD 60.

Mark is said to have composed his Gospel in

Rome, based on Peter's teachings, so it would have been written before Peter's martyrdom there in AD 68.

John, the only Gospel *actually* composed after AD 70 (it was written around AD 85–90), doesn't even bother to repeat Jesus' prophecy about the destruction of the temple—whereas, according to the skeptics, it would have been the most likely to.

> **ArchaeoLogic:** Jesus said that not one stone of the temple would be left upon another (Mark 13:2), and this was fulfilled. The present-day Wailing Wall wasn't part of the temple, but is the remains of a wall that surrounded the western courtyard of the temple.

19. Different Audiences and Approaches

The Gospel writers wrote with different audiences or purposes in mind, so they approached the same subject matter from different perspectives.

Historians estimate that in the first century AD, there were eight to ten million Jews of the Diaspora scattered throughout the Roman Empire. Few spoke Hebrew or Aramaic. The vast majority spoke and read only Greek. So when Matthew wrote his Gospel, it wasn't only for the Jews in Israel. He also had this larger Jewish audience in mind. That's why he repeatedly demonstrated that Jesus was the Messiah who had fulfilled the Old Testament prophecies.

But the Gospel of Matthew was too distinctly Jewish for many Gentiles—and it *was* the larger Gentile audience that Luke was writing for. They not only spoke and read Greek but also understood the world from a Greek worldview. Among other things, they had a concept of an "ideal man," so Luke stressed Jesus' love, compassion, and humanity.

It has often been said that Mark was writing for the action-focused Romans because he used the word *immediately* so often. However, it's also likely that Mark refrained from adding parables, stories, and lengthy teachings because he was intent on creating a short, easily grasped account of Jesus' life for both Romans *and* Greeks.

According to the church fathers, when John was old, the bishops of Asia Minor asked him to compose a Gospel that would oppose the heresies of Cerinthus (an early Gnostic) as well as the Ebionites (Hebrews who believed that Jesus was the Messiah but not the divine Son of God). So John related stories that stressed, more than any other Gospel writer, the deity of Christ.

> **ArchaeoLogic:** The Greek word *politarchs* (city rulers) used in Acts 17:6, 8 for the rulers of Thessalonica, doesn't appear anywhere in Greek literature, causing scholars to doubt Luke. But in 1835 the word was found inscribed on an arch on the west side of Thessalonica.

20. Paul's Thirteen Epistles

The four Gospels make up 46 percent of the New Testament. The next-largest group of books are the epistles (letters) written by the apostles. The apostle Paul penned thirteen of these over a seventeen-year period. He wrote his first letter, 1 Thessalonians, about AD 51, and his last one, 2 Timothy, around AD 68, shortly before his martyrdom.

Paul didn't write the epistle to the Hebrews, however. The writing and oratory style are clearly not his. It also doesn't contain Paul's standard greeting, "Grace to you and peace from God our Father and the Lord Jesus Christ" (Romans 1:7 NKJV). Who wrote it? Tertullian thought that Barnabas, Paul's fellow apostle, had. Martin Luther suggested that Apollos (Acts 18:24–28; 1 Corinthians 3:4–8) was the author.

In modern times, it's been popular for textual critics to assert that the three Pastoral Epistles (1 and 2 Timothy, and Titus) weren't written by Paul either. They base this claim largely on the usage of a few words that don't appear in Paul's previous epistles. However, the style and contents of these last three epistles *are* clearly Pauline, and they were accepted as such by the early Christians. (And they all contain variants of his standard greeting.)

The minor differences can be explained by the fact that after writing the first ten epistles, Paul was released from his first Roman imprisonment and traveled to Spain in the far west of the Empire to preach the Gospel. This new cultural experience, plus the passage of some years, and the different focus of these epistles, well account for the differences.

> **ArchaeoLogic:** Jeremiah 34:7 states that when the Babylonians were besieging Jerusalem, only Lachish and Azekah also remained. In 1935 and 1938, eighteen messages were found at the ancient city mound of Lachish. One of them records that the fire signals of Azekah have gone out.

21. The Writing of the Rest

There are seven other epistles in the New Testament. Jesus' half brother James, who had risen to prominence as a leader of the Jewish Christians, wrote one of them. The epistle of James was probably composed around AD 60, although some date it to AD 50. Jude, also Jesus' half brother, wrote a short epistle probably before AD 65. Peter also wrote two epistles—1 Peter in the early AD 60s, and 2 Peter between AD 65 and 68.

The apostle John wrote in his later years. He didn't write the Gospel of John until about AD 85–90. He also wrote three short epistles (1, 2, and 3 John) between AD 85 and 95, and the book of Revelation after his release from exile in AD 96. Eusebius, the leading Church historian, states that John was sent to Patmos during Emperor Domitian's persecution, and released by Emperor Nerva, who reigned from AD 96 to 98.

Some scholars believe that the apostle John didn't write Revelation: the Gospel of John is written in correct, polished Greek, whereas the grammar in Revelation is often written like a barbarian (non-Greek). Greek wasn't John's mother tongue, but the Muratorian fragment states that he had help composing his Gospel, and internal evidence supports this (see John 19:35; 21:24). However, John recorded Revelation alone after a major persecution.

This same answer applies to Peter's epistles: critics insist that an uneducated Galilean fisherman couldn't have written the polished Greek of 1 and 2 Peter. But Peter was helped by a Christian fluent in Greek. He declared: "With the help of Silas. . .a faithful brother, I have written to you" (1 Peter 5:12 NIV).

What Was Included and What Was Not

22. The Scriptures in Jesus' Day

When Jesus referred to verses from the Old Testament, He called them the Word of God or the scriptures, which means "the writings." The Law of Moses had existed in written form for nearly fifteen hundred years. After giving the Law, God had inspired the Jews to write books of history, psalms, and proverbs and had sent numerous prophets speaking His Word. The Jews referred to this entire collection of scripture as the Law and the Prophets (Matthew 7:12) or the Law, the Prophets, and the Psalms (Luke 24:44).

But which writings were considered scripture, and which were not—and when was the canon of scripture closed? Is it true that the Jews never formally ratified their canon of scripture until the Council of Jamnia around AD 90—some sixty years after Jesus? And does that mean (as skeptics assert) that the Jews hadn't agreed on what was scripture *before* this date?

Such theories were common in the last century, but have fallen into disrepute since the 1960s. The Jamnia hypothesis is now considered dead. Only two books were discussed at this council—Ecclesiastes and the Song of Solomon. Whether at this council or during this general era, the rabbis also rejected the Septuagint translation and any books that hadn't been originally written in Hebrew, such as the pseudographic books of the Apocrypha.

The entire canon of the Jewish scriptures was already established by Jesus' day. Malachi, the last book of the Prophets, was written around 430 BC, and all the books in our present Old Testament had been accepted as inspired and were in common use by 200 BC.

> **ArchaeoLogic:** Archaeologists have discovered that in Jesus' day, Nazareth was an insignificant village of some fifty houses covering a mere four acres. This is the context for Nathanael's derogatory question: "Can anything good come out of Nazareth?" (John 1:46 NKJV).

23. The Apocrypha Rejected

All the books of the Old Testament were originally written in Hebrew—with portions of Daniel, Ezra, and Jeremiah in Aramaic. The Jews zealously guarded these sacred scrolls, and as previously mentioned, a specialized class of scribes arose to make accurate copies of the Hebrew scriptures. They continued making copies centuries after Hebrew was no longer commonly spoken by the Jews. The four hundred years between Malachi, the last book in the Old Testament, and Christ—when God wasn't speaking—are called "the four hundred silent years."

They weren't exactly silent, however, but were filled with the chatter of noncanonical writers who were busy writing books in Greek, not Hebrew or Aramaic. Some of these writings contained factual history and moral truths, but many of them were outright fabrications—purporting to have been written in Hebrew by ancient authors like Baruch and Enoch, whereas they were actually recent forgeries written in Greek.

Many of these ended up in the Greek Septuagint, which was translated from the Hebrew between 285 and 132 BC. Because these spurious books existed in Greek already, they didn't seem out of place. But the leading rabbis were never confused. If copies of a book didn't exist in Hebrew in the scrolls in their possession, they knew it wasn't canonical. It wasn't actually scripture. In the end they rejected such books because they had never accepted them in the first place.

The books of the Apocrypha still appear in Catholic and Orthodox Bibles, but aren't accepted as canonical by Protestants—for the same reason that the rabbis didn't accept them.

24. Jesus' Words
Equated with Scripture

In the beginning, all Christians were Jewish, and to these first disciples the Word of God meant the Hebrew scriptures. But very early on in Jesus' ministry His disciples realized that He was the Messiah, the Christ. As Peter confessed, "You have the words of eternal life. Also we have come to believe and know that You are the Christ, the Son of the living God" (John 6:68–69 NKJV).

God had spoken about a great Prophet that He would send one day (Deuteronomy 18:15–19), saying: "I will put my words in his mouth" (v. 18 NIV). Jesus stated, "I have given to them the words which You [God] have given Me" (John 17:8 NKJV). The first Christians knew that Jesus was this Prophet (Acts 3:22–23) and the Messiah. This meant that His words were the very words of God—on the same level as the already-accepted scripture.

This is why the book of Acts repeatedly refers to the apostles preaching "the word of God" (Acts 6:7; 11:1; 12:24; 13:5; 17:13; etc.). It was only natural that if preaching the Gospel (the story and words of Jesus) was accepted as equal to the scriptures, that the written versions of the Gospels would also be considered scripture.

In AD 63–65, Paul referred to the written sayings

of Jesus on the same level as the Law of Moses. He stated, "For the Scripture says, 'You shall not muzzle an ox while it treads out the grain,' and 'The laborer is worthy of his wages'" (1 Timothy 5:18 NKJV). The first passage Paul quoted was Deuteronomy 25:4. The second passage was Luke 10:7.

> **ArchaeoLogic:** In Acts 18:2 (NKJV) Luke writes that "Claudius had commanded all the Jews to depart from Rome." Roman historian Suetonius said that the AD 49 expulsion of Jews was a result of them rioting over "one Chrestus." Latin speakers often mistook Christus (Christ) for Chrestus.

25. The Epistles Recognized as Scripture

Christians also recognized that Jesus, by the Holy Spirit, had spoken through the apostles. This is hardly surprising. Jesus had, after all, specifically commissioned His apostles to preach the Word and to bear witness of Him. So Paul wrote, "If anyone thinks himself to be a prophet or spiritual, let him acknowledge that the things which I write to you are the commandments of the Lord" (1 Corinthians 14:37 NKJV). The apostle Peter acknowledged this very thing.

Peter had read Paul's epistles, and wrote in AD 65–68, "Bear in mind that our Lord's patience means salvation, just as our dear brother Paul also wrote you with the wisdom that God gave him. . . . His letters contain some things that are hard to understand, which ignorant and unstable people distort, as they do the other Scriptures, to their own destruction" (2 Peter 3:15–16 NIV). Peter first mentions Paul's letters then in the same breath talks about "the *other* Scriptures," clearly equating the two.

In the same epistle, Peter included himself and the other apostles as those whom Jesus had spoken through and given commands. He said: "I want you to recall the words spoken in the past by the holy prophets and the command given by our Lord and Savior through your Apostles" (2 Peter 3:2 NIV).

The book of Revelation, written by the apostle John, begins with these words: "This is a revelation from Jesus Christ" (Revelation 1:1 NLT). We see then that at the very time of writing, Jesus' apostles declared their writings to be inspired by God—and within a few years they were explicitly recognized as scripture.

26. The New Testament Canon

The synoptic Gospels were referred to as scripture in AD 63–65, and the first ten epistles of Paul (written before AD 62) were accepted as scripture by AD 68. But what was the earliest Bible canon, the list of accepted inspired writings?

No list per se survives from the first century, but in his epistle, Clement, bishop of Rome (about AD 96), quoted Paul's letters and Hebrews; and Ignatius, bishop of Antioch (about AD 110), quoted Paul's letters, Acts, and the Gospels of Luke and Matthew. Papias called Mark a true Gospel around AD 110. Polycarp, also writing around AD 110, quoted from all of the above writings, as well as from 1 and 2 Timothy, 1 Peter, and 1 John.

During the following decades, copies of other writings were widely distributed and recognized as inspired. Valentinus, who taught around AD 130–160 and was a Gnostic, in order to impress orthodox Christians, quoted the Gospel of John and 1 John (as well as James and Revelation) in a manner that showed he accepted them as authoritative.

The church leader Irenaeus (AD 130–200) quoted from all of the Gospels and the epistles of Paul. The Muratorian fragment (a canon by the church in Rome around AD 170) accepted virtually all the books in our New Testament, including Jude and Revelation. It also says that in addition to his first ten epistles, Paul wrote "one to Titus, and two to Timothy; and these are held sacred in the esteem of the Church."

In AD 367, Athanasius, bishop of Alexandria, listed the exact same books we have today.

> **ArchaeoLogic:** The Rylands Library Papyrus P52 is a papyrus fragment containing fourteen lines from the Gospel of John. Its strong Hadrianic style dates it to AD 117–138. John's Gospel was written in Ephesus about AD 85–90 and copies existed in Egypt within a few years.

27. Accepting Books into the Canon

Some people wonder why it took until AD 367 for the church to make up its mind which books were inspired, and which weren't. This question gives the impression that *most* of the canon of scripture was unsettled for 333 years after Jesus' death. The truth, however, is quite different.

The four Gospels, Paul's first ten epistles, Acts, 1 John, and 1 Peter were recognized as scripture by AD 140, meaning that more than 84 percent of the New Testament was accepted by that date. When Titus and 1 and 2 Timothy were recognized as inspired by AD 170, the canon of the New Testament was 87 percent settled—actually, 94 percent settled, since the Muratorian canon also listed Jude and Revelation ("the Apocalypse of John").

Notwithstanding, in AD 300, Eusebius wrote, "Those that are disputed, yet familiar to most, include the epistles known as James, Jude, and 2 Peter, and those called 2 and 3 John." He said about Revelation that while "some reject it, others include it among the Recognized Books" (*Ecclesiastical History*, bk. 3, ch. 25). Although *some* rejected Revelation, every previous source had quoted it or referred to it as inspired.

And despite the fact that the epistle to the

Hebrews was one of the last books to be accepted (by the Eastern churches, that is, largely because they didn't know who had written it), Clement had quoted it around AD 96, it was cited as scripture around AD 140, and accepted and published with Paul's epistles in the Beatty Papyrus P46, which dates AD 175–225.

28. Gnostic Writings Rejected

Gnostics called themselves *gnostikoi*, from the Greek word *gnosis*, which means "knowledge" or "the act of knowing." Gnostics appeared some sixty years after Christ. Their myths drew heavily from the treatise *Timaeus* by Plato, and by AD 130 they had fully developed their theology. They wrote their spurious "gospels" in the second century AD, claiming that they'd been written earlier by Thomas, Mary Magdalene, Philip, John, Judas, and others.

There were several varying systems of Gnostic belief, but according to a main one, the first thing the true God (Monad) created was Barbelo; then He created ten aeons; then He created Christ. Everything was fine until a goddess named Sophia (Wisdom) arranged a self-induced pregnancy and had a deformed son called Ialdabaoth (a.k.a. the Demiurge or devil).

A basic belief of all Gnostics was that only spiritual things were good. Therefore the "god of the Jews" who created the evil physical earth was not the true God, but Ialdabaoth. The world was corrupt and human bodies were prisons; therefore the Gnostic gospels describe Christ as a disembodied spirit imparting "secret knowledge" to help people escape this life.

Most Gnostics were moral people, usually celibate; they even frowned on simple pleasures like enjoying food. The Cainites, however, were a Gnostic sect who counted Cain and Judas Iscariot as heroes. Since the "evil god of the Jews" had commanded men not to commit sexual immorality, the Cainites preached wild sexual behavior to disobey him (see *Against All Heresies* by Irenaeus). The Gospel of Judas was one of their religious texts.

The leaders of the early church easily recognized these writings as nonhistorical frauds, and therefore excluded them from the New Testament.

> **ArchaeoLogic:** In AD 180, the Christian bishop of Lyons, Irenaeus, wrote a treatise condemning the Gospel of Judas, but the actual text of the Gospel wasn't known. Then, in 1983, a copy of it in the Coptic language, carbon dated to about AD 280, was smuggled into Switzerland and sold.

Scribes and Scribal Errors

29. The Inerrant Original Autographs

The Word of God, as originally given in the Old and New Testaments, contains no false statements or mistakes. God doesn't lie (Numbers 23:19). God doesn't make mistakes. As Paul tells us, "All Scripture is given by inspiration of God, and is profitable for doctrine, for reproof, for correction, for instruction in righteousness" (2 Timothy 3:16 NKJV). Since the Bible is inspired directly by God, and isn't merely something dreamed up by men, it's an eminently trustworthy source for establishing Christian doctrine.

"Above all, you must realize that no prophecy in Scripture ever came from the prophet's own understanding, or from human initiative. No, those prophets were moved by the Holy Spirit, and they spoke from God" (2 Peter 1:20–21 NLT; see also 1 Thessalonians 2:13).

However, while Evangelical scholars affirm that the Bible is "inerrant in its original autographs" (the manuscripts written by the original authors), they recognize that over the centuries as the scriptures were copied by hand, minor scribal errors crept into the text. The surviving copies of the Hebrew and Greek texts aren't entirely free of *human* error.

Although the scribes took great care when copying the scriptures, they occasionally made mistakes. The vast preponderance of these are obvious spelling errors, the accidental dropping of a word, copying the same line twice, etc. These kinds of mistakes present little challenge to scholars, as the original wording is never in doubt. And even in the case of unusual "textual variants" (variations or differences in the text) many thousands of copies of the scriptures exist—some of them very early—which experts can check variants against.

30. Copying the New Testament

In the early decades when the Gospels and other writings initially circulated singly, they were likely copied by available literate Christians. However, by about AD 140, two factors would have led to trained scribes making the copies: First, Christians are known to have preferred the new codex (book) format over scrolls by then. The Rylands Library Papyrus P52 (dated AD 117–138) of John's Gospel is from such a codex. Codices made it practical to preserve writings in larger units. Second, 84 percent of the New Testament had been accepted as scripture by that date, and copying that much sacred text would have been an important, carefully executed undertaking, best done by professionals.

At first, the New Testament was preserved in four separate codices: (1) the four Gospels made up one volume; (2) the epistles of Paul and Hebrews comprised a second; the Beatty Papyrus P46 (AD 175–225) is an example of this second volume; (3) Acts and the other epistles were together in a third book; and (4) Revelation was its own volume.

Regarding the second, Pauline volume, scholars believe that—before sending his epistles to churches—Paul had copies made for personal reference. His first ten epistles were then compiled into a single document, probably by AD 61, because it wasn't certain Paul would be released from house arrest (Acts 28:30)—though he was. This is why the first ten epistles of Paul existed as one unit from the earliest times. Titus and 1 and 2 Timothy were added to this codex soon after.

In AD 331, Constantine ordered the Christian scholar Eusebius to produce fifty copies of the Bible (including the New Testament) in large codices, and professional scribes were employed for this task—and would be from then on.

> **ArchaeoLogic:** The Tel Dan Stele is an inscribed stone found at the ancient city mound of Dan in northern Israel in 1993–1994; the inscription, written in Aramaic and likely done by order of Hazael king of Aram, commemorates a victory over the "house of David."

31. Examples of Scribal Errors

The main reason there are so many minor textual variants, despite the likelihood that professional scribes handled copying from an early date, is that there are more than 5,600 copies of Greek New Testament manuscripts in existence. That amounts to some *1.3 million* pages of text! Small wonder that there are a large number of scribal errors. But let's be clear: most of these mistakes are insignificant and don't change the meaning of the text.

What kinds of mistakes did scribes make? Well, they sometimes spelled words wrong. These don't change the meaning, however. All they show is that scribes—like many people today—had a habit of misspelling certain words.

They sometimes lost their place while copying: this happened when two subsequent lines of text ended with the same letter. The scribe would think that he had already copied the second line, so he skipped over it. This kind of mistake is obvious wherever it occurs.

Certain Greek words sound almost the same, though the meanings are different. Thus, when a reader was reading aloud to several scribes in a scriptorium, one scribe might write down the wrong word.

Scribes would confuse word order. In English this is a big deal, as there's a huge difference between

"Silas told Phoebe" and "Phoebe told Silas." In Greek, however, this isn't an issue, because the meaning of a phrase doesn't depend on word order, but on the inflection added to word endings. So you could write, "told Phoebe Silas," and a Greek reader would still understand clearly that it meant "Silas told Phoebe" if Silas had a *nominative* ending and Phoebe had an *accusative* ending.

32. Unquestioned Christian Doctrine

You often hear Christian apologetics experts say words to this effect: "Despite the textual variants in Greek copies of the New Testament, not one important Christian doctrine is affected or called into question." What do they mean by that, and is it accurate?

Yes, it's accurate. What it means is that even if a reading in one Greek manuscript is the result of a scribal error or an unwarranted emendation (correction), that particular verse is not the only place such a teaching appears. Vital doctrines do not rise or fall on one mention alone.

For example, the Byzantine text, on which the King James Version and the New King James Version are based, quotes John the Baptist as saying: "And I have seen and testified that this is the Son of God" (John 1:34 NKJV). The eclectic Greek text behind the New International Version (and *most* modern translations) reads: "I have seen and I testify that this is God's Chosen One" (John 1:34 NIV).

Does the doctrine of the deity of Christ collapse if "Son of God" is *not* the original wording in John 1:34? Hardly. The Greek text behind the NIV proclaims this same truth in countless other places (see Matthew 8:29; 14:33; 16:16; Mark 1:1; 3:11; 15:39; John 1:49; 3:18; 5:25; 11:27; 20:31; Acts 9:20;

Romans 1:4, 9; etc.).

The same applies to the doctrine of the Trinity: the King James Version contains a clear declaration of the trinity in 1 John 5:7–8, but almost no other translations have it. Again, the doctrine of the Trinity remains solid, even if, as many Christians claim, this phrase started out as a scribe's marginal note and was later mistakenly incorporated into the text.

> **ArchaeoLogic:** There are more than 5,600 extant copies of Greek New Testament manuscripts. About twelve come from the AD 100s, sixty-four date back to the AD 200s, and forty-eight copies were made in the AD 300s. Together, these earliest copies contain the complete New Testament several times over.

33. Higher and Lower Criticism

Some Christians, when they hear the terms *higher criticism* of the Bible or *lower criticism* of its text, think that all such criticism is derogatory and involves a negative attack on the veracity of scripture. This *is* frequently the case, but literary criticism literally means to make sound, logical deductions based on the evidence.

Higher criticism is the attempt to establish the author of the original text, as well as the date and place of writing. A valid use of higher criticism is to observe that the Greek of Hebrews is markedly different than the Greek in Paul's epistles—then to seek to determine who wrote Hebrews, if not Paul. An example of unwarranted higher criticism driven by agenda is scholars insisting that Moses couldn't have written the Law in the 1400s BC, but that it was fraudulently cobbled together by nameless editors. . .one thousand years later!

Lower criticism (textual criticism) attempts to determine the original text where scribal errors have created differences. By closely comparing ancient copies, textual critics seek to identify mistakes and restore the correct word. Legitimate textual criticism is very useful, and helps clear up questions about what the original autographs said.

But again, lower criticism is often employed by skeptics to attempt to "prove" that the text of the

Bible is inaccurate, or is so full of mistakes that it's untrustworthy. They examine the text armed with presuppositions that even innocent scribal errors were deliberate changes, theologically motivated— whereas there are often simple, alternate explanations that make a great deal of sense.

Making Sense
of Supposed
Contradictions

34. The Gospels versus Paul's Epistles

Many people, after reading the synoptic Gospels then the epistles of Paul, get the impression that they're two very different messages. The Gospels tell the story of Jesus' life, crucifixion, burial, and resurrection, and for the most part contain teachings on how to live a righteous life. Consider Jesus' statements in the Sermon on the Mount, for example.

Paul does talk about living a righteous life, but he stresses that Jesus is the Son of God; he repeatedly teaches that we must believe on Jesus to be saved, and that we're not saved by our own righteousness, but by God's grace. Many lay people—and a number of scholars—therefore argue that Paul changed the Gospel into something Jesus never preached and never intended.

Two important Bible books disprove this fallacy and provide bridges between the synoptic Gospels and Paul's epistles. First, the book of Acts shows clearly that *all* early Christians preached that Jesus saves us by grace alone. (Read Acts 2:37–38; 4:12; 5:29–31;

9:19–20; etc.) The apostle Peter summed up the entire early Church's position, saying, "We believe it is through the grace of our Lord Jesus that we are saved" (Acts 15:11 NIV).

Second, the Gospel of John declares like Paul that Jesus is the Son of God, equal to God, and that salvation is only in Him (see John 3:3–7, 16; 6:28–29, 40; 8:24; 10:30; 14:6; etc.). John summed up his message saying: "But these are written that you may believe that Jesus is the Messiah, the Son of God, and that by believing you may have life in his name" (John 20:31 NIV).

> **ArchaeoLogic:** Scholars used to doubt Acts 18:12 that Gallio was proconsul (governor) of Achaia, but in the early twentieth century an inscription was found at Delphi; it was a copy of a letter by Emperor Claudius to "Lucius Junius Gallio, my friend, and the proconsul of Achaia."

35. The Synoptics and John's Gospel

The Gospel of John doesn't retell most of the events of Jesus' life mentioned in the other Gospels, such as His birth, His baptism, or His temptation. In fact, it doesn't mention most of the healings and other events that all three synoptic Gospels describe Jesus performing in Galilee. It does, however, describe *other* healings and miracles Jesus did—mostly in Judea. Plus, it recounts many new incidents and conversations. Fully 90 percent of the material in John's Gospel is new.

But John doesn't contradict Matthew, Mark, or Luke. Rather, it's a rich source of information that fills in many gaps in the story. When synchronized with the synoptic Gospels, it gives us a fuller picture of the timeline and events. For example, the synoptic Gospels don't say how much time passed between Jesus' baptism and His crucifixion. You might think that His entire public ministry lasted only one year. The Gospel of John, however, mentions several Jewish feasts—including a number of Passover feasts. This is how we're able to determine that Jesus' ministry lasted about three and a half years.

John also emphasizes the deity of Christ to a much greater extent than the other Gospels. While this theme *is* found in them, John repeatedly states it.

Because of this, some critics argue that the theology of John's Gospel is so "highly developed" that it must have been written after John by a "Johannine community." But Jerome wrote that one of the reasons John wrote his Gospel was to counter the heresies of the Ebionites, who taught that Jesus was the natural son of Joseph who had *become* the Son of God at His baptism.

> **ArchaeoLogic:** Critics in the 1900s contended that John's Gospel wasn't an accurate historical source. This was disproved in 2004 when Jerusalem city workers, excavating a sewer pipe, discovered the Pool of Siloam mentioned in John 9:7. It was as large as two football fields.

36. Differences in Details

Skeptics seek to point out contradictions between the synoptic Gospels—Matthew, Mark, and Luke—since they contain the same overall story and many of the same details. Critics are often motivated by the belief that if they can find even the smallest contradiction between them, then none of the Gospel story need be trusted—absolving them from any responsibility to obey it. After all, they claim, the Gospels aren't divinely inspired but merely the writings of mere fallible men, so it should come as no surprise that they're full of mistakes and inconsistencies.

Even Christians who aren't motivated by unbelief are sometimes perplexed and even troubled when they read what seem to be contradictions in the accounts. The difference is that they trust that there must be logical explanations—and the good news is that there are.

Often, two conflicting statements can be reconciled simply by looking a little deeper into the meaning of the original Greek words. Also, knowledge of biblical geography and customs can help clarify what the original writer meant or *didn't* mean. Bible dictionaries and study helps are good in that they contain the solutions to many common conundrums.

In the case of the Synoptics, it helps to understand

that the writers of the Gospels all had access to a large body of written records and eyewitness perspectives about the various stories—all of which were true, but which contained more information about incidents than any one writer included in his Gospel. By combining and reconciling these differing details, we get a better picture of what happened than we can by reading just one Gospel.

> **ArchaeoLogic:** Jesus often spoke in the synagogue in Capernaum (Mark 1:21). In 1968, under the ruins of a synagogue, an *earlier* synagogue with a similar floor plan was found; in 1981 its basalt floor was uncovered, and pottery on it was dated to the first century.

37. When Jesus Called His Disciples

Mark's Gospel says that as Jesus walked by the Sea of Galilee, He saw Simon and his brother Andrew fishing, said, "Follow Me," and that they immediately left their nets and followed Him. Then He saw James and John, called them, and they, too, dropped everything and followed Him (Mark 1:16–20 NKJV).

However, in his Gospel, John doesn't mention this event. Instead, he says that Simon and Andrew met Jesus many miles to the south along the Jordan River (John 1:35–42). Which account is right? They both are. In fact, the details in the Gospel of John help Mark's account make sense. Many people assume that Simon and Andrew (and James and John) had never seen Jesus before, but that when He called them to follow Him, they inexplicably left all to do so. But in real life, people don't blindly follow total strangers.

Simon and Andrew had first met Jesus along the Jordan River and were the "we" who went back north with Him to Galilee (John 1:43–45). They were among His disciples who accompanied Him to Cana (John 2:1–2). When Jesus did a miracle there, they believed in Him (John 2:11). Then they returned to their fishing, and talked about Him nonstop to their business partners, James and John.

When Jesus called them to follow Him around Galilee, they did (Mark 1:16–20). After a while, when back in Capernaum, they returned temporarily to their regular jobs. Jesus then astonished them by doing another miracle (Luke 5:1–11) and called them to follow *full-time*. They believed in Him and knew Him well enough to follow without hesitation.

38. One Person or Two?

Jesus and His disciples crossed the Sea of Galilee to Gentile territory. As the boat beached, two demon-possessed men came out of the hillside tombs, shouting at Him. Jesus cast out the demons, they entered a herd of pigs, and the pigs rushed headlong into the lake and were drowned (Matthew 8:28–34). It's a dramatic story that shows the power that Jesus has over evil spirits. Mark 5:1–20 and Luke 8:26–39 tell the same story as Matthew, with one difference: they only mention *one* demon-possessed man. So how many *were* there?

There were two; however, one man was clearly the leader and the spokesperson. He was also outstanding in other ways: after the demons were cast out of both men, one man apparently left while the other not only stayed but also earnestly asked Jesus to let him follow Him full-time. He later went out and enthusiastically proclaimed Jesus to his entire region. Small wonder that Mark and Luke focused on him!

(Note: this same principle applies when Matthew 20:29–34 tells us that Jesus healed two blind men near Jericho, but Mark 10:46–52 lists only one, Bartimaeus.)

Another point about the former demoniac: Matthew 8:28 (NIV) says that this incident happened in "the region of the Gadarenes," whereas Mark and

Luke both say that it took place in "the region of the Gerasenes." Which is right? They both are. The capital city of this whole region was Gerasa, some thirty-seven miles southeast of the Sea of Galilee, whereas the incident happened in the *immediate* region of a city named Gadara, a mere six miles away.

> **ArchaeoLogic:** The small town of Gadara (modern Kursi) was near the east shore of the Sea of Galilee. It's the only location on this shore with a steep bank, which the herd of pigs plunged down. The herdsmen then ran into the nearby town of Gergasa (Mark 5:13–14).

39. Differences in the Resurrection Accounts

While the important facts of Jesus' resurrection are the same, the four Gospels describe different combinations of women going to His tomb, seeing and hearing and doing slightly different things. Some people give up trying to arrange a probable order of events—but this is one of the most rewarding Bible studies imaginable. When all four witnesses come together, a beautiful and realistic picture emerges.

Several factors must be taken into consideration: First, all four accounts have clearly been contracted into brief narratives with all the women named together, yet there were clearly two groups of women that morning setting out from separate locations. One group was led by Mary Magdalene (John 20:1); the other was led by another of Jesus' prominent female disciples (Luke 8:1–3; 24:10; Mark 16:1).

It also helps to clarify the order of events if you bear in mind that Mary Magdalene told Peter and John the news first, then *later* told the main group of apostles. John owned a house nearby, in Jerusalem, and he and Peter were there that morning (John 18:15–16; 19:26–27; 20:1–3). The other disciples (except for Thomas) had apparently retreated to Bethany, two miles distant, where they had previously stayed (Matthew 21:17; 26:56; John

20:24). So Mary and the women reported to two different groups in succession.

Also, the tomb was near the city (John 19:20, 41), so it didn't take long to go there and back. Mary Magdalene is known to have visited the tomb twice (John 20:1–11) and apparently went back a third time with the other Mary (Matthew 28:9–10). There was a great deal of excited running around that morning.

40. Jesus Cleansing the Temple

One of the "contradictions" people most commonly point to is that all three synoptic Gospels describe Jesus driving the money changers out of the temple courts in AD 30, at the very end of His ministry—just days before He was crucified. After riding a donkey into Jerusalem, "Jesus entered the temple courts and drove out all who were buying and selling there. He overturned the tables of the money changers and the benches of those selling doves" (Matthew 21:12 NIV; see also Luke 19:28–46; Mark 11:1–17).

The text of John's Gospel only repeats 10 percent of the material in the synoptic Gospels, so it's not surprising that he doesn't mention Jesus clearing out the temple in AD 30. What does raise eyebrows, however, is that John tells us that Jesus did this exact same thing three years earlier in AD 27 (John 2:13–16). To many skeptical scholars, this is clear-cut proof that John mixed events up, so they declare that the Gospel of John can't be trusted.

On the contrary, when you look closely at the details and do a little math, the case for John's trustworthiness is even stronger. After Jesus cleared the temple in John's account, the Jews stated that the temple had been forty-six years in the building thus far (John 2:20 NIV). Secular history tells us that Herod began to rebuild the temple about 20 BC. That puts the date of this incident at AD 26–27.

And as already mentioned, the temple cleansing in the synoptic Gospels happened in AD 30.

Conclusion: Jesus cleared out the temple in AD 27 and *again* in AD 30.

> **ArchaeoLogic:** Luke mentions the prohibition against Gentiles entering the Jewish temple (Acts 21:27–29). Archaeologists have discovered two stone slabs, written in Latin and Greek, warning Gentiles not to enter the restricted temple area upon pain of death.

41. Searching Out Answers

We don't have space in this book to deal with every Bible difficulty, but as mentioned before, there are study helps that deal with many of the most common questions. *The NIV Study Bible* is an excellent place to start. There are also good resources on the Internet. If you have a question about something, it's likely that a number of other people have noticed it before you, have given a great deal of thought to it, and have written about it.

In fact, Christian thinkers have been dealing with some of the same questions since the earliest days. For example, you may have noticed that the major events of Jesus' ministry in the Gospels are in the same chronological order, but sometimes the minor incidents have been arranged differently. The church father Tertullian (AD 160–220) wrote his view on this: "Never mind if there does occur some variation in the order of their narratives, provided that there be agreement in the essential matter of the faith" (*Against Marcion*, IV, 2).

Sometimes that's the approach to take: questions about the order of events in the Gospels can be particularly challenging at times, and though you may arrange the available data and come up with a plausible chronology, there's sometimes simply not enough evidence to be able to nail down an ironclad conclusion. At times like that, Tertullian's advice is still the best.

Also, when the Gospels give varying accounts of the same incident, know this: the event described actually *happened*, and happened in such a way that blends the details that the different Gospel writers give.

The Bible Makes Ultimate Sense

42. Creation Not Blind Chance

In recent decades, one of the most hotly contested issues has been the question of origins—and with good reason. After all, the opening words of Genesis are an emphatic statement: "In the beginning God created the heavens and the earth" (Genesis 1:1 NKJV). The Bible declares not only that there is an all-powerful God but also that He created everything that exists—from distant galaxies to the smallest life-forms on earth.

Critics have focused on this issue: if they believe that science proves that the Bible is wrong on this one crucial point, then it follows that it's wrong on all other points. Or, even if the Bible happens to be correct on most other points, they become irrelevant. If it's mistaken about this foundational statement, they believe that enough of their case is made that the discussion is over.

In fact, many people adopt this attitude: if God didn't create all that we see around us—but the laws of physics can account for the existence of all matter and energy, and blind chance and evolution can explain the rise of life—then whether God exists or not is beside the point. If He didn't create the world, if He's not going to answer their prayers, and they disagree with what He states about moral issues, then they might as well ignore Him.

This isn't the motivation of all unbelievers; many are sincerely unconvinced that the Bible is correct on the issue of origins. But for far too many, belief in classical neo-Darwinian evolution (even if they can't explain it) makes a handy peg to hang their hats on.

> **ArchaeoLogic:** According to Genesis, Nahor was the brother of Abraham and a "city of Nahor" existed near Haran (Genesis 11:27; 24:10). This city is also mentioned in texts from Mari in the nineteenth century BC; it was near Haran in the Balikh River valley of southern Turkey.

43. Christian Views on Creation

The main Christian views on Creation are as follows: Young-earth creationism is the traditional view of the Church, stating that six to ten thousand years ago, God created the universe in six literal days; that there was a global flood; and that Genesis 1–10 is an accurate historical record, intended to be taken at face value.

Old-earth (progressive) creationists also believe that God created all life forms, but agree with radiometric dating methods that show that the earth is 4.5 billion years old. They reason that the *days* of Genesis were successive ages, during which God did progressive acts of creation. They note that the fossil record testifies to the sudden appearance of new, fully developed life forms, not to missing links or transitional forms.

The gap theory is so named because its proponents believe that there's a gap between Genesis 1:1 (when earth was created 4.5 billion years ago) and verse 2. They believe that the fall of Satan marred creation and was why "the earth was without form, and void" (Genesis 1:2 KJV; see also Jeremiah 4:23–26). Then six thousand and some years ago, God re-created the earth and life.

Other Christians favor theistic evolution: they believe that God is responsible for the rise of life, but that evolution is the mechanism He used to produce its many varying forms. Rather than holding to neo-Darwinian theory, however, many argue that the evolutionary process supports the concept of deliberate design.

Intelligent Design (ID), for its part, seeks not so much to explain *how* God created everything as it does to focus on the fact that life itself gives evidence of intelligent, intentional design.

44. Proof of an Intelligent Designer

The Bible says: "The heavens proclaim the glory of God. The skies display his craftsmanship. . . they make him known" (Psalm 19:1–2 NLT). Cosmologists and physicists agree that the forces of nature are specifically tweaked to be in a very narrow range that's favorable to life. If the laws of physics were weaker or stronger by more than a fraction of 1 percent, stars and galaxies couldn't have formed, and matter itself might not have been able to come into existence. Scientists call this principle the "fine-tuned universe."

And not just the heavens overhead, but the earth beneath our feet and all around us teems with life that gives evidence for an Intelligent Designer. They make God known. This is especially true when we investigate life at the microbiological and molecular levels.

Neo-Darwinian evolution states that genetic information changes randomly; everything is one grand, blind experiment, with the vast majority of mutations being harmful to DNA. But they contend that the rare mutation is beneficial and is passed on to succeeding generations. But pro-ID biologists ask, "Do earth's complex life forms show evidence for blind chance being the catalyst, or do they show evidence of purposeful design?"

One area where the evidence favors Intelligent Design over Darwinian evolution is "irreducible complexity." This is where several interacting components all contribute to the function of an organism, and where eliminating one component doesn't create a simpler, more primitive form, but causes the entire organism to cease functioning. This is true with organs like the eye and with the workings of cells. There are no transitional, less-complex forms.

> **ArchaeoLogic:** Minimalist archaeologists argue that an urban society (an actual kingdom) only came into being in Judah in the eighth century BC or later. Recent excavations at Khirbet Qeiyafa (a Judean site occupied 1050–970 BC) clearly show that one existed in the eleventh century BC.

45. Christianity Is True and Reasonable

Nearly two thousand years ago, the apostle Paul was explaining to the Roman governor Festus how Jesus had fulfilled ancient prophecies that foretold that the Messiah should die then rise again. Festus had listened patiently up to this point, but this was too much. He interrupted, "You are out of your mind, Paul! . . . Your great learning is driving you insane." Paul responded, "I am not insane, most excellent Festus. . . . What I am saying is true and reasonable" (Acts 26:24–25 NIV).

This is an important point. After the divine intervention of creation, skeptics have the most difficulty accepting that God raised Jesus from the dead. Secular scientists don't believe in miracles and automatically discount them, even when a miracle is the best explanation for an event. They contend that Christians aren't being rational to believe such things.

Neo-Darwinian evolutionists often attack pro-ID biologists simply because they have faith in a Creator; they insist that their "religious bias" disqualifies their scientific opinions. But pro-ID biologists use accepted scientific methods to conduct their experiments, and their conclusions are based on solid empirical evidence. It's good science, whether it lines up with the worldviews of secular scientists or not.

And whether a phenomenon can be explained and understood, if it actually happened, it actually happened. Any explanations as to *how* it happened have to follow along as best they can. And Jesus *did* rise from the dead. More than five hundred witnesses attested to this fact. This is why Paul could say that what he was testifying about was true. But the Christian faith is not only true; it is also reasonable.

ArchaeoLogic: According to Roman records, Porcius Festus was indeed procurator (governor) of Judea; he ruled from about AD 59–62. Many bronze coins called prutah, minted by Porcius Festus, are in existence. If you're a coin collector you can buy one starting at about $25.

46. Taking the Maker's Instructions Seriously

The problem many people have with accepting that God created us is that it automatically establishes His authority over us. It means we must take His commands seriously. Even people who know little about the Bible are aware of the Ten Commandments, and know they're not obeying one or more of them. Or they suspect that they're living in violation of other biblical laws. And if they have even a passing knowledge of the New Testament and know that Jesus commanded us to love our enemies, they're *certain* that they're falling short.

They realize that if they accept God's Word as authoritative, they're obliged to try to obey it—and they know that in most cases this will mean a radical change of lifestyle. Many people are honest enough to realize that they don't want to give up their selfish habits. Or they may have been exposed to legalistic, uncharitable forms of Christianity in the past, and view all Christians as hypocrites. Whatever their excuses or reasons, they have little desire to live what they think is an overly righteous lifestyle.

And yet, if they pause to think about it, a natural progression of logic continues to impress itself on their minds: (a) there is a significant amount of evidence that God must exist; (b) most people are also persuaded that God—though perhaps a bit distant and austere—is a good God; (c) He has set in place good moral laws for our own benefit and for the benefit of others; and (d) it is therefore incumbent upon us to obey these laws.

47. Life after Death— and Judgment

Most North Americans believe in God, believe that the human spirit survives the death of the physical body, and believe in heaven or some kind of afterlife. The percentages change from year to year, but generally more than 90 percent of Americans polled say that they believe in God, a supreme spiritual Being. Those questioned range from dedicated Christians to the uncommitted.

Also, 75 percent say that they believe in life after death. But here's where things start getting vague for many people. In a 2012 poll, 40 percent of Americans said they believed in life after death but not in heaven or hell. And it's not that they all believe in reincarnation or some other alternate spiritual state instead. They believe that the spirit lives on, but simply can't say *what* the afterlife is like.

In many cases, this is because their minds have rejected the concept of a loving God sending sinners to an eternal, fiery hell. But though we may not understand what form such punishment may take, and whether the biblical imagery is literal or symbolic, it logically follows that if God created moral laws and we're commanded to obey them, and if our spirits one day go to meet God, that's when we'll give an account for our actions on earth. The

Bible, in fact, speaks of this event and calls it the Judgment.

We know that God is a loving God, that He is merciful, but that He is also just and all-knowing; He will punish sin. However He judges, "the judgments of the LORD are true and righteous altogether" (Psalm 19:9 KJV).

ArchaeoLogic: Sodom and Gomorrah were destroyed when burning sulfur rained down on them (Genesis 19:24). Bab edh-Dhra, southeast of the Dead Sea, was also destroyed by an earthquake and fire that began *on the rooftops*. The ruins are covered by a layer of spongy ash four to twenty inches deep.

---

48. Is Eternal Hellfire Reasonable?

Jesus warned that the unrighteous would be "cast into hell fire—where 'their worm does not die and the fire is not quenched'" (Mark 9:47–48 NKJV). John wrote that the wicked "shall be tormented with fire and brimstone" and that "the smoke of their torment ascends forever and ever" (Revelation 14:10–11 NKJV). Many Christians take this imagery quite literally.

Other Christians believe that literal, never-ending torment in a lake of fire and burning sulfur is inconsistent with the fact that God is love (1 John 4:8). Eternal punishment seems unreasonable. So they consider this imagery to be symbolic. Billy Graham said that he thought that the fire was a burning thirst for God that can never be quenched. He added, "I think that hell. . .is separation from God forever." In other words, people end up not going to heaven because they reject the truth then later regret their decision for all eternity.

Others believe that hell is more tangible but doesn't literally last "forever." Jesus was quoting Isaiah 66:24, which speaks about dead bodies burning outside Jerusalem. And John was paraphrasing Isaiah 34:9–10, which describes God's judgment on the land of Edom: "Its land shall become burning pitch....Its smoke shall ascend forever."The Edomites *were* judged and no longer exist, yet their land didn't actually burn forever.

Some Christians conclude that whatever punishment God metes out, it matches the crime and has a limit (Luke 12:47–48). They believe that the unsaved are consumed in hell, and that experiencing the "second death" (Matthew 10:28; Revelation 21:8) means that they literally cease to exist.

ArchaeoLogic: Jesus referred to hell as *Gehenna*, a place where worms (maggots) fed on rotting corpses and fires burned (Mark 9:47–48). *Gehenna* comes from *ge-hinnom* (Valley of Hinnom). It was Jerusalem's garbage dump—a place where the dead bodies of criminals were often burned.

---

49. What You Must Do to Be Saved

Many people avoid following a line of reasoning that leads to belief in a day of Judgment. They do this by maintaining a vague concept of God, by espousing the belief that all religions are valid paths to Him, and by assuming that they're living moral enough lives to make it into whatever heaven hopefully exists.

Regarding the first two points, Jesus declared, "I am the way, the truth, and the life. No one comes to the Father except through Me. If you had known Me, you would have known My Father also. . . . He who has seen Me has seen the Father" (John 14:6–7, 9 NKJV).

All vagueness about what God is like disappears when we realize that Jesus Christ, as seen in the Gospels, is the perfect "image of the invisible God" (Colossians 1:15 NIV). He's not only a *perfect* way to God, but as He stated, He's the *only* way. The Bible says: "Believe on the Lord Jesus Christ, and you will be saved" (Acts 16:31 NKJV).

And *why* must we believe on Jesus to be saved? Because God calls us to live perfect lives, obeying His commandments, loving Him with all our hearts, and loving our fellow man as much as we love ourselves. But we all fall short of this high standard (Romans 3:23). We simply can't be good enough to "earn" our way into heaven—so God sent Jesus to die on the cross to take our punishment. If we accept Jesus' sacrifice, instead of being judged for our sins, we're forgiven and freely inherit heaven.

Why Obeying God Makes Sense

50. The Highest Moral Teachings on Earth

Jesus summed up all the laws and moral codes of the Old Testament when He said, "The most important commandment is this: 'Listen, O Israel! The LORD our God is the one and only LORD. And you must love the LORD your God with all your heart, all your soul, all your mind, and all your strength.' The second is equally important: 'Love your neighbor as yourself.' No other commandment is greater than these" (Mark 12:29–31 NLT).

Jesus also said, "So in everything, do to others what you would have them do to you, for this sums up the Law and the Prophets" (Matthew 7:12 NIV).

The New Testament also declares a powerful truth: love is not only the foundation of *our* relationship with God and one another, but also the foundation of who God is and His relationship with us—for "God is love" (1 John 4:8 KJV). God embodies all that love is. Love is what motivates the all-powerful Creator in everything He does. In fact, His great love was the reason He sent Jesus into the world: "For God so loved the world that he gave his one and only Son, that whoever believes in him shall not perish but have eternal life" (John 3:16 NIV).

Jesus' teachings are the highest moral laws on earth. Now, the concept of a faith based on love is not unique in today's world. Many new religious groups preach love as a central tenant of their belief system, but they merely borrowed this idea from Jesus' teachings. This goes to show that they recognized the truth of His words.

> **ArchaeoLogic:** Pilate is mentioned in the Gospels, and by the historians Josephus and Tacitus. His historicity was confirmed in 1961 by the discovery of the Pilate Stone, a limestone block, in Caesarea; this inscription mentions "Pontius Pilate. . .the Prefect of Judea."

51. The Foundations
of True Life

Loving God, and loving our neighbors as ourselves, are the foundations of true life. We obey these commandments because God said so, but there are common-sense reasons to live these principles as well. First, we're told, "You must love the LORD your God" (Mark 12:30 NLT). But what *causes* us to do this spontaneously and sincerely?

The Bible tells us: "We love him because he first loved us" (1 John 4:19 KJV). God loved us before the thought ever occurred to us to love Him. God shows us that He loves us by providing for our physical needs, through people who love us, and by giving us joy and beauty in our lives. And He shows His great love by giving us eternal life through His Son, Jesus Christ. Realizing that God cares for us so much causes us to love Him.

Knowing, truly knowing, that God loves us also gives us peace of mind and calms our worries and fears—which gives us a sense of well-being. This in turn affects our mental and physical health. Love has great power. "There is no fear in love; but perfect love casts out fear. . . . He who fears has not been made perfect in love" (1 John 4:18 NKJV).

Second, we're told, "Love your neighbor as yourself" (Mark 12:31 NLT). When you love others as much as you love yourself, you seek to do only good to them. "Love does no harm to a neighbor" (Romans 13:10 NIV). When you love people, you try not to hurt them, defraud them, gossip about them, and so on. Love is the foundation for true life.

52. Radical Principles Make Good Sense

Many people have difficulty seeing the sense in some of Jesus' more radical teachings. For example, He commanded us to love our enemies, and said that if someone slaps your face, you should offer the other cheek as well. If someone forces you to walk one mile carrying his load, you should freely offer to go two miles (Matthew 5:38–41).

These teachings are counterintuitive. They seem to make no sense. You can understand being civil around nasty people—to keep from causing yourself trouble, if nothing else—but why go out of your way to let others take advantage of you? Why choose to cheerfully show *love* to someone who means you nothing but ill? Jesus explained:

"But I say, love your enemies! Pray for those who persecute you! In that way, you will be acting as true children of your Father in heaven. For he gives his sunlight to both the evil and the good, and he sends rain on the just and the unjust alike" (Matthew 5:44–45 NLT). You are to love your enemies because God loves them; you belong to Him, and He wishes you to show them His love. This may not change their hearts immediately, but it makes good sense in the long run—and has a positive impact on your own life.

Also, notice that Jesus said to walk two miles with someone, not twenty. He said to love and pray for your enemies, not allow them to do you harm. And His point about letting someone slap both cheeks was that you shouldn't seek to inflict pain on someone in revenge—especially over small offences.

ArchaeoLogic: Mark 10:46–42 says Jesus healed blind Bartimaeus while *leaving* Jericho, but Luke 18:35–43 says it was while *entering* Jericho. There were two Jerichos— the old city (now Tell es-Sultan) and a new city (now Tulul Abu el-Alayiq), built by Herod a mile to the south.

---

53. Not Caring Just for Yourself

Jesus taught financial principles that run counter to our natural, self-preserving instincts, but that make perfect sense when seen within a larger context. For example, He said, "Give to everyone who asks of you" (Luke 6:30 NKJV), and added that if anyone wants to borrow something from you, you shouldn't turn him or her away (Matthew 5:42).

Many people think that they'd be picked clean if they dared live such an open policy. But the apostle Paul clarified what this meant: "Of course, I don't mean your giving should make life easy for others and hard for yourselves. I only mean that there should be some equality. Right now you have plenty and can help those who are in need. Later, they will have plenty and can share with you when you need it" (2 Corinthians 8:13–14 NLT).

Jesus was not teaching impractical generosity, and Paul was not teaching communism. They were exhorting Christians to live the caring, supportive lifestyle already found in loving, functional families, whose members look out for one another in times of need. Jesus' teachings against covetousness, hoarding, and materialism remind us that we have an obligation to our spiritual family—our Christian brothers and sisters—and, in fact, to all people.

It was in this context that God commanded, "You shall not harden your heart nor shut your hand from your poor brother, but you shall open your hand wide to him and willingly lend him sufficient for his need. . . . And your heart should not be grieved when you give to him, because for this thing the LORD your God will bless you in all your works" (Deuteronomy 15:7–8, 10 NKJV).

54. Living with an Eternal Perspective

God commanded His people to willingly lend to the poor and to not be grieved when they gave. The reason many people hesitated to lend, and grieved when they did, was because of a very real concern that the poor might not be *able* to pay them back. From a practical perspective, it seemed like a risky venture. It didn't make financial sense.

But God promised to bless them for it. The Bible added: "He who has pity on the poor lends to the LORD, and He will pay back what he has given" (Proverbs 19:17 NKJV). They weren't losing even if the poor never repaid the money. God saw to it that they were repaid somehow.

Most people anticipated receiving material blessings or health or protection or success in this life, but Jesus took things a step further, saying that not all rewards are given in the here and now. As He told one rich, young ruler, "Give to the poor, and you will have treasure in heaven" (Mark 10:21 NIV).

Jesus taught the greater value of heavenly treasures when He said, "Lay not up for yourselves treasures upon earth. . . . But lay up for yourselves treasures in heaven" (Matthew 6:19–20 KJV). Any wise financial planner will tell you that to reach your long-range goals, you must be willing to make lifestyle adjustments and make certain sacrifices in the short term. Since we only live a few decades in this mortal world, but will spend the rest of eternity in heaven, it makes perfect sense to invest heavily in our eternal future.

> **ArchaeoLogic:** In 2011, archaeologists recovered a stolen ossuary (small box for human bones) with the inscription: "Miriam, daughter of Yeshua, son of Caiaphas, Priest of Ma'aziah." Caiaphas was the Jewish high priest who had sat in judgment on Jesus (Matthew 26:57–65).

55. The Measure
of True Success

On the one hand, unbelievers criticize wealthy Christians for not giving enough to the poor and worthy charitable causes; on the other, they look down on poor, struggling Christians (trying to live principles of generous giving and financial honesty) as not being practical or shrewd enough to achieve material success. Some openly mock a belief in heavenly rewards, calling it wishful "pie in the sky."

They also point out that Christians, who they think are supposed to be blessed and prosper because they live for God, aren't always spared life's hard blows. Christians suffer from illnesses, accidents, financial problems, and setbacks like everyone else. And many times they suffer persecution and are ostracized because they follow Jesus. So outsiders ask what's the value in being a Christian?

Many of these same people hunker down into a self-centered lifestyle, and measure their success by this standard: "He who has the most toys when he dies, wins." Jesus, however, bluntly contradicted this when He said, "Take heed and beware of covetousness, for one's life does not consist in the abundance of the things he possesses" (Luke 12:15 NKJV). The media is full of stories of celebrities who have achieved phenomenal "success"—wealth, notoriety, and all that their hearts could desire—only to have everything come crashing down, victims of their own excess and out-of-control lifestyles. Jesus asked, "For what shall it profit a man, if he shall gain the whole world, and lose his own soul?" (Mark 8:36 KJV).

To find true meaning in *this* life and to inherit *eternal* life is to truly succeed—however you fare in this world.

Is the Bible Still Relevant Today?

56. Christianity Enlightens Society

To its most vocal critics, Christianity is a backward religion from the Dark Ages, whose outdated, intolerant teachings are holding back progress and human rights. But a look at history shows that the exact opposite is true. In the centuries after Jesus, Christianity spread through the Roman Empire, challenging the dominant pagan belief system and the social order of its day. Not only did it set people free spiritually, but since it is a faith based on love and self-sacrifice, it also corrected many abuses:

The New Testament declared slaves equal to nobles in God's eyes, and Christians led the drive to eventually abolish slavery altogether. Female infanticide was common amongst the Romans, with newborns left exposed to die; Christians rescued and adopted these abandoned babies. And much of our modern social consciousness came into being because Jesus' followers generously supported widows, orphans, and the disabled.

Even when they were a despised underclass, Christians willingly supplied emergency aid to victims of natural disasters such as earthquakes and famines, as well as social upheaval. After they came to power, Christians outlawed the cruel gladiatorial blood sports. Beginning in AD 325, they founded hospitals in every large city of the Roman Empire. Christians created orphanages, homes for the poor and the elderly, soup kitchens, and prison ministries.

Jesus' teachings have had a profound impact on society, and gave birth to most of the enlightened ideals and compassionate institutions that we now take for granted in the modern world. Christianity's critics should be aware that these sweeping advances have come about as a direct result of putting the New Testament into practice.

> **ArchaeoLogic:** Paul wrote from Corinth, "Erastus, the treasurer of the city, greets you" (Romans 16:23 NKJV). In 1929, archaeologists in Corinth found this inscription on a marble paving stone: "Erastus, commissioner of public works, bore the expense of this pavement."

57. Christianity and Religious Pluralism

America has always been a nation of immigrants, and in recent decades has become home to millions more people of diverse cultures, traditions, and religious beliefs. People who once lived in distant lands are now our neighbors, our classmates, and our coworkers. As followers of Jesus, we are to love them without prejudice or discrimination. We are also to respect them and their right to hold their beliefs.

We can believe in *cultural pluralism*—where groups within a larger society maintain their unique cultural identities without fully assimilating—but not believe in *religious pluralism*, which means accepting all religions as equally valid. But proponents of religious pluralism usually aren't content to agree to disagree. They say that we must agree that everyone else's beliefs are as valid as faith in Jesus because it is "their truth."

This worldview is so pervasive that even many nominal Christians believe it. It is, of course, illogical, since many religions are mutually exclusive. Jesus said, "I am the way, the truth, and the life. No one comes to the Father except through Me" (John 14:6 NKJV). The apostle Peter added, "Salvation is found in no one else, for there is no other name under heaven given to mankind by which we must be saved" (Acts 4:12 NIV).

Just because the Bible is no longer read in public schools, doesn't mean that it's any less true. Just because America is no longer officially a Christian nation doesn't mean that the biblical principles on which it once stood have weakened. God's Word remains true, however many people disbelieve it. Modern religious pluralism hasn't superseded the Bible's authority.

58. Are Parts of the Bible Outdated?

Many of God's laws in the Old Testament are eternal truths, such as the Ten Commandments (Exodus 20:1–17). These have not become outdated. But parts of the Law such as the ritualistic laws of Leviticus are no longer in effect.

The Law of Moses gave detailed instructions on how to perform animal sacrifices to cover sin. It also gave many laws about ritual purity that Christians don't practice today. So have the Old Testament commandments been abolished? No. Jesus said, "Do not think that I have come to abolish the Law or the Prophets; I have not come to abolish them but to fulfill them" (Matthew 5:17 NIV).

"For the law, having a shadow of the good things to come, and not the very image of the things, can never with these same sacrifices, which they offer continually. . .make those who approach perfect" (Hebrews 10:1 NKJV). The Law was a foreshadowing of the reality to come—Jesus. He completely fulfilled the Law's requirements when He died on the cross. He was the perfect, ultimate sacrifice, "the Lamb of God who takes away the sin of the world" (John 1:29 NLT; see also Galatians 3:24–25).

Jeremiah wrote that the days were coming when God would make a *new* covenant with His people

(Jeremiah 31:31–34), and the writer of Hebrews pointed out that "by calling this covenant 'new,' he has made the first one obsolete; and what is obsolete and outdated will soon disappear" (Hebrews 8:13 NIV). When the Jewish temple, where blood sacrifices had to be made, was destroyed by the Romans in AD 70, the entire old sacrificial system did indeed disappear.

> **ArchaeoLogic:** The Samaritans worshipped God on Mount Gerizim (John 4:19–24) and built a temple there in the early fifth century BC. They built a second temple over that around 200 BC, and the Jewish leader John Hyrcanus destroyed it in 128 BC. Archaeologist Yitzhak Magen has uncovered the remains of both buildings.

59. The Bible's Eternal Truths

Many people feel not only that portions of the Old Testament no longer relevant today, but also that much of what the New Testament says is passé—especially when they don't happen to agree with certain statements.

However, what the Bible says about humankind's need for salvation still holds true because people are still sinners, and still unable to save themselves. Two thousand years ago, faith in Jesus was the only way to be saved, and that hasn't changed, because "Jesus Christ is the same yesterday, today, and forever" (Hebrews 13:8 NKJV).

The command for Christians to love one another hasn't changed either—and never will. After all, it's one of the defining marks of being a Christian. Jesus said, "By this everyone will know that you are my disciples, if you love one another" (John 13:35 NIV).

The New Testament's declarations about sexual morality haven't changed either. Much of modern society is reverting to the pre-Christian sexual promiscuity of the Greeks and Romans (1 Peter 4:3–4), but this doesn't mean that the Bible is outdated. It simply shows that it's easier to give in to fleshly desires than to exercise self-control.

However, certain parts of the New Testament were written within a specific cultural context, and aren't necessarily practiced by Christians today. For example, Paul instructed believers to "greet one another with a holy kiss" (Romans 16:16 NKJV). This was the standard greeting back then—and still is in some cultures—but most Christians today are more likely to give a handshake or a hug. The essence of the principle is what's important here.

60. Does the Bible Promote Slavery?

If Christians recognize that slavery is morally repugnant—and if Christians were the ones who championed the emancipation of slaves—then why did the apostle Paul condone the institution in his epistles? For example, he wrote: "Slaves, obey your earthly masters in everything you do. Try to please them all the time, not just when they are watching you. Serve them sincerely" (Colossians 3:22 NLT). So was slavery a sanctioned institution?

No. These statements were made within a specific cultural context. Slavery in the Roman Empire in Paul's day was harsh at times, but not as harsh as what later existed in America. Emperor Claudius (before AD 54) ruled that a master who killed a sick or worn-out slave could be charged with murder. When Paul wrote to the Colossians about slavery in AD 60, Nero (in his saner days) had just granted slaves the right to lodge complaints against their masters in a court of law for unfair or cruel treatment.

This is not to say that slavery was a desirable state even then. But Paul couldn't openly call for empire-wide emancipation without being arrested and executed for stirring up a slave revolt. But he advised, "Were you a slave when you were called? Don't let it trouble you—although if you can gain your freedom, *do so*" (1 Corinthians 7:21 NIV, emphasis mine).

And in a letter to a wealthy Roman friend, Philemon, Paul not only asked him to forgive a runaway slave named Onesimus, but also requested that he set him free: "He is no longer like a slave to you. He is more than a slave, for he is a beloved brother.... Welcome him as you would welcome me" (Philemon 1:16–17 NLT).

> **ArchaeoLogic:** Herod Antipas founded the new city of Tiberias around AD 20, but because he built it on top of tombs, pious Jews refused to live there. So Herod populated it with foreigners. Great numbers of slaves were freed under the condition that they would settle in Tiberias.

61. Does All the Bible Apply to Us?

Jesus fulfilled the Law and the Prophets, and the new covenant superseded the old covenant, but this didn't mean that the Old Testament scriptures were no longer profitable to read. They had, after all, been purposefully given by God. Paul reminded Christians: "All Scripture is given by inspiration of God, and is profitable for doctrine, for reproof, for correction, for instruction in righteousness" (2 Timothy 3:16 NKJV). *All* scripture is profitable.

Even though the Law was simply a foreshadowing of the reality of Christ, there is much to be learned from it. Even though some precepts are no longer in effect, the deeper truths behind them, the spiritual principles embodied in them, are still true.

Paul demonstrated how the principle behind an ancient agricultural law also applied in his day and age to those who did the Lord's work—they had a right to earn a living from their labor. Paul explained, "For it is written in the Law of Moses: 'Do not muzzle an ox while it is treading out the grain.' Is it about oxen that God is concerned? Surely he says this for us, doesn't he?" (1 Corinthians 9:9–10 NIV).

And we can be inspired by the courage and faith of the Old Testament characters, as well as be warned by the bad examples of the unfaithful. In

1 Corinthians 10:1–10, Paul briefly mentions five different examples of what happened to the children of Israel in the wilderness, then says, "These things happened to them as examples for us. They were written down to warn us who live at the end of the age" (1 Corinthians 10:11 NLT).

62. Why You Should Read Your Bible

There are several good reasons to read your Bible. First of all, it teaches you how to acquire spiritual life. Jesus said, "It is the Spirit who gives life. . . . The words that I speak to you are spirit, and they are life" (John 6:63 NKJV).

Second, the Gospel is "the word of his grace, which is able to build you up" spiritually (Acts 20:32 KJV). Paul wrote to the early Christians, "You didn't think of our words as mere human ideas. You accepted what we said as the very word of God—which, of course, it is. And this word continues to work in you who believe" (1 Thessalonians 2:13 NLT).

A third reason to study the scripture is so that you can know what it actually *says*, and *doesn't* say. Many people who have never read the Bible imagine that it says things like, "All religions are a true path to God." Of course, it says nothing of the sort. Jesus warns such people, "You are in error because you do not know the Scriptures" (Matthew 22:29 NIV).

If you've never read your Bible, then the best place to start is in the four Gospels, the story of Jesus. Then go on to read the entire New Testament. Many people begin in Genesis and find that easy enough reading, but then quickly get bogged down in the ceremonial laws and detailed history of the following books. You will also find much valuable reading in the books of Psalms and Proverbs. After you've read the New Testament two or three times then, yes, start reading the Old Testament at the beginning.

> **ArchaeoLogic:** Jesus often taught in the temple courts (John 10:23), and pilgrims ascended stone steps to reach the courts from the south. Teachers often spoke from these steps to crowds in the square below. Archaeologists uncovered the largest of these sets of steps in 1968, still intact.

Understanding the Bible

63. Sincerely "Searching the Scriptures"

If you're investigating Christianity to see if it makes sense, it helps greatly if you're prepared to abandon your presuppositions. We all have worldviews through which we sift evidence. Sometimes we construct these mind-sets out of a sincere pursuit of the truth; other times they're born of selfish or faulty reasoning—or clouded by prejudice or emotions.

Presuppositions include a number of assumptions. If you've witnessed Christians acting hypocritically, or living self-centered lifestyles, you might have arrived at the conclusion that all Christians are hypocrites. If a Christian has ever given simplistic answers to your questions, you might assume that the Bible has no answers. Or perhaps you assumed that all Christians believe in a certain brand of Creationism—one that you don't find convincing.

If you're willing to drop such presuppositions, reexamine the evidence for God, then you'll be ready to go where it leads—and there *is* significant evidence.

Paul preached the Gospel in Thessalonica then

in Berea, and the Bible commended the Bereans, saying, "These were more fair-minded than those in Thessalonica, in that they received the word with all readiness, and searched the Scriptures daily to find out whether these things were so" (Acts 17:11 NKJV). Note that they didn't simply accept everything Paul said, but checked it out for themselves. But they *did* check it out.

Apart from checking the scriptures to ascertain that they're a sensible guide for life, check out the wealth of archaeological evidence for the Bible; check out the scientific evidence for intelligent design; check out the statistical improbability of the Bible's many prophecies being fulfilled by mere chance.

64. Interpreting the Bible

This same Berean principle holds true if you're a Christian and someone teaches a doctrine you've never heard before: search the scriptures. Be fair-minded. Be *ready* to believe, but don't be gullible. "Only simpletons believe everything they're told!" (Proverbs 14:15 NLT).

The Bible says the gullible are "tossed to and fro, and carried about with every wind of doctrine" (Ephesians 4:14 KJV). Rather than being blown about like a tumbleweed, dig deep in your search for answers, sink your roots down into the most important, foundational truths of the Bible—to love God with all your heart and your neighbor as yourself—and you'll be "rooted and grounded" in the truth (Ephesians 3:17 NKJV).

On the other extreme, some Christians cling to doctrinal positions even when they know (or ought to know) that there is evidence to the contrary. For example, they might believe in "prosperity doctrines" and desire for God to bless them financially so much that they ignore the fact that believers are warned against the desire to be rich (1 Timothy 6:5–10)—or the fact that many Christians lived their faith to the full and were blessed even though they experienced "deep poverty" (2 Corinthians 8:2 KJV).

A Jewish expert once grilled Jesus on how to

gain eternal life. Jesus in turn asked him, "What is written in the law? What is your reading of it?" (Luke 10:26 NKJV). There are two questions here: Jesus wanted to hear what *he* thought the most relevant, important scriptures were; the verses the man focused on showed his priorities. Jesus' second question was to probe what the man understood those scriptures to mean.

ArchaeoLogic: Jesus' hands and feet were pierced by nails (Luke 24:39), but skeptics used to doubt that Romans drove nails through feet. Then, in 1968 the bones of a crucified man named Jehohanan were discovered with nail marks in both wrists and the seven-inch spike still in his heels.

---

65. The Most Important Doctrines

As you read the Gospels and the entire New Testament, it becomes readily apparent that they were written to inform you of many truths that you are to believe and put into practice. While I could supply a detailed list of the most basic doctrines all Christians should agree on, this has already been done in creeds such as the Nicene Creed, many centuries ago.

The Gospel writers declared what they considered to be the most essential truths when they wrote, "These are written that you may believe that Jesus is the Christ, the Son of God, and that believing you may have life in His name" (John 20:31 NKJV). Believing this is the heart of the Gospel, since truly *knowing* God is what gives you eternal life (John 17:3; 1 John 4:15).

Believe that and you won't have much problem believing other truths such as the virgin birth or the need to live a moral life. Christians, to be saved, also must believe that Jesus rose from the dead (1 Corinthians 15:12–14), but again, if you sincerely believe that He's the Son of God, you shouldn't have any issues with this biblical truth as well.

Mere mental assent that there's a God, or that Jesus was a real, historical person, is not enough, however. Even the devils believe that (James 2:19).

As Jesus stressed, to truly possess eternal life, you must *love* God with all your heart and soul and strength and mind, and you must *love* your neighbor as yourself (Luke 10:25–28). To truly know God is to love Him and others (1 John 4:7–9).

66. Disagreeing on Secondary Issues

There is a great deal of diversity between churches—from differing doctrines to varying styles of worship and music. Often, these differences are superficial: one church believes most things another church believes, but chooses to emphasize certain beliefs or practices. Other times, Christians are divided by well-defined doctrinal differences. Most of the time, fortunately, they agree to disagree, and accept one another as fellow Christians. This is as it should be. We *are* free to disagree on secondary issues. Paul wrote:

"Accept the one whose faith is weak, without quarreling over disputable matters. One person's faith allows them to eat anything, but another, whose faith is weak, eats only vegetables. The one who eats everything must not treat with contempt the one who does not, and the one who does not eat everything must not judge the one who does, for God has accepted them. . . . One person considers one day more sacred than another; another considers every day alike. Each of them should be fully convinced in their own mind" (Romans 14:1–3, 5 NIV).

Of course, when it comes to foundational doctrines or basic moral teachings, it's important to "contend earnestly for the faith" (Jude 1:3 NKJV). This is true when people promote teachings or "revelations" that pervert or drastically alter the focus of biblical Christianity. For example, Jude spoke out against the teaching that Christians were free to engage in flagrant sexual promiscuity (Jude 4, 17–19; see also 1 Corinthians 6:13–20).

The mistake Christians sometimes make, however, is to "contend earnestly" with other Christians over minor disagreements. Along with zeal, we need both wisdom and love.

ArchaeoLogic: Could Christians eat meat from the meat market (*macellum*) that had been offered to idols? Paul, writing to the Christians in Corinth, answered this in 1 Corinthians 8:1–13; 10:25–30. Archaeologists have found a Latin inscription identifying a Corinth meat and fish market.

---

67. Learning about the Bible

There are several ways to learn the Word of God, and all of them are important. If you wish to persevere in your faith and to understand the Bible, an excellent way is to attend a church. Not only will you be encouraged by fellowship with other believers, but you can also hear Bible-based sermons. A good preacher will do as Paul told Timothy: "devote yourself to the public reading of Scripture, to preaching and to teaching" (1 Timothy 4:13 NIV).

But you won't survive—or at least not become a mature Christian—by hearing the Word only one hour a week, no matter how good the preacher is. You must read the Bible yourself, pausing to meditate on its truths and praying for ways you can apply them to your life. Most of what you read will be easy to understand, though not always easy to live.

However, if you're not familiar with Bible geography, history, culture, and prophecy, you can feel lost at times. A Christian named Philip once asked a man who was reading the prophet Isaiah, "Do you understand what you are reading?" "How can I," the man answered, "unless someone explains it to me?" (Acts 8:30–31 NIV). That's where it helps to read books that give basic introductions to the Bible and Bible times.

Finally, it can be educational to join a Bible study group where someone is teaching, but you get a chance to interact, ask questions, and discuss. "They read from the Book of the Law of God and clearly explained the meaning of what was being read, helping the people understand each passage" (Nehemiah 8:8 NLT).

68. It's Okay to Ask Questions

When you don't understand something in the Bible, or if something appears to be a contradiction, ask questions. Often you can resolve the issue if you pursue it with persistence (Proverbs 2:3–5). So consult Bible help books, research on the Internet, and ask knowledgeable Christians. It's important to have sincere questions answered so that they don't fester in the back of your mind and turn into doubts.

Thomas is often called "doubting Thomas" because he didn't believe at first that Jesus had risen from the dead. He wasn't there when Jesus appeared to His disciples, and though they insisted that it was Him, Thomas figured they'd just seen Jesus' spirit. Thomas said he'd have to put his fingers in Jesus' wounds before he'd believe He had physically come back to life. And Jesus gave him that opportunity (John 20:24–29).

But what many people don't realize is that when the other ten disciples first saw Jesus, they had the *same* questions. They just didn't *ask* them. So Jesus Himself asked, "Why do doubts arise in your hearts?" (Luke 24:36–39 NKJV). Then, to prove that He wasn't a spirit, He showed them His nail wounds and commanded them to touch Him. They were so overjoyed that they still wondered if they could trust their senses—so He offered *more* proof by eating in front of them.

Now, some spiritual mysteries are beyond the ability of our limited minds to comprehend, but this is *not* the case with most questions people have about the Bible. In most cases it's "ask, and it will be given to you; seek, and you will find" (Matthew 7:7 NKJV).

ArchaeoLogic: Jesus said, "The scribes and the Pharisees sit in Moses' seat" (Matthew 23:2 KJV). This was a seat in the synagogue where the Law of Moses was read. In 1926, a "Seat of Moses," carved from basalt, was found at the ancient synagogue of Chorazin, Galilee.

Making Sense of a Suffering World

69. Why Does God Allow Suffering?

Many people are troubled by the question of how a God of love could cause or allow all the suffering that happens in the world. The Bible states that "God is love" (1 John 4:8 KJV) and declares that He is all-powerful: "Behold, You have made the heavens and the earth by Your great power. . . . There is nothing too hard for You" (Jeremiah 32:17 NKJV).

Yet to many people, both statements can't be true. They conclude either that He is all-powerful—since He created the entire universe—but like an absentee watchmaker, He stands distant from humankind's woes because He doesn't care, or they reason like Rabbi Harold Kushner (who wrote *When Bad Things Happen to Good People*) that God does care, but He isn't quite all-powerful.

A third position is that all suffering is a result of a holy God judging sin. Every volcanic eruption or earthquake or epidemic happens because God is judging people for their collective sins. When one person gets sick, it's a judgment on that individual's sin. To many people, this is an overly judgmental concept of God. Plus, it doesn't explain why God *doesn't* judge hundreds of millions of equally bad people.

A fourth explanation, based upon Job's example (Job 1–2), is that all disasters, disease, and suffering happen when God allows Satan to afflict humankind—often for reasons that seem mysterious and inexplicable to us. Ultimately, suffering happens because God personally gave permission for it to happen (Exodus 4:11; Isaiah 45:7).

So which view is correct? Actually, there's some truth in most of them, since any one position by itself can be overly simplistic.

70. Humanity's Self-Inflicted Suffering

Atheists, agnostics, and Christians can all agree on one basic point—that humankind's selfishness and ignorance is the cause of most human suffering. Deforestation and unwise agricultural methods cause erosion and desertification. Pollution poisons our planet's soil, water, and air. Wars driven by bigotry and greed cause death, destruction, and suffering— not only for combatants, but also for innocent civilian populations.

In addition, the actions of unscrupulous corporations directly contribute to economic recession, putting millions out of work. Promiscuous sex is the main reason for the spread of STDs. Countless traffic fatalities are the result of speeding, reckless driving, or driving under the influence. Illegal drug usage results in personal misery, crime, and even plunges entire nations into deadly drug wars. The list goes on and on.

The majority of humankind's suffering is self-inflicted. The principle of cause and effect is at play, and when it comes to bringing suffering upon ourselves, the Bible says, "Whatever a man sows, that he will also reap" (Galatians 6:7 NKJV). And yes, at times this principle includes God directly intervening in our circumstances and ensuring that trouble comes upon us.

But this isn't a hard-and-fast principle that can be applied to all, or even most, situations. Not all trouble or sickness is a result of God judging sin. If so, the most wicked people would be quickly and severely punished. Yet as David observed, God *didn't* always immediately judge them for their sins and oppression of the poor; instead, they continued to prosper and live easy lives. But, as he realized, they *would* get their just dues in the end (Psalm 73:1–19).

> **ArchaeoLogic:** Paul spent three years in Ephesus, and today much of the Roman city he knew so well has been excavated— including the amphitheater where a riot raged for more than two hours (Acts 19). The theater, the largest in the ancient world, could seat about 44,000 people.

71. Earthquakes, Volcanoes, and Tsunamis

Many Christians believe that God created the world in pretty much the state that we presently find it. So they have no explanation for why earthquakes, volcanoes, and tsunamis happen, other than that they're direct acts of God to punish humankind for sin. Most earthquakes, however, are too small to cause damage and can only be picked up by seismological instruments.

So what causes these things? Plate tectonics is a good explanation. Science tells us that the earth's outer layer (lithosphere) is broken up into seven to eight large plates, and that these plates are slowly moving, driven by the spreading ocean floor and large convection currents in the earth's mantle. Where plates collide, mountain ranges such as the Himalayas are thrust up. Where one plate slides under another, mountains are built through volcanic activity; Japan and the Andes Mountains are examples of this.

The enormous pressures from the sliding and colliding plates are released in bursts of energy called earthquakes. If earthquakes happen at sea, they can cause tsunamis. Most of earth's active volcanoes exist in the Ring of Fire on the edges of the Pacific plate. So these natural disasters aren't caused by God's continual intervention.

However, God is perfectly able to make earthquakes happen. He had His people settle in Canaan right beside the Arabian tectonic plate (the cause of the Jordan Rift Valley), so they experienced lots of earthquakes. Some of these were huge and destructive (Amos 1:1), and some were just big enough to shake things up and were timed to draw people's attention to what He was doing (Matthew 27:50–54; 28:1–2).

72. Disease and Medical Conditions

When we or our loved ones are stricken with diseases such as cancer, or suffer from debilitating medical conditions, we often assume that God is punishing us for some sin, or we ask, "Why me?" Why, we wonder most of all, are innocent children randomly born with rare diseases?

We know that germs and viruses are responsible, together with faulty or damaged genetic codes, and that an inactive lifestyle and poor diet are often the catalysts for illnesses. But while we can take responsibility for our dietary and exercise choices, the questions remain: If God exists, why did He create viruses in the first place? If He designs everyone from birth, why give some people DNA that causes them to be born with medical conditions?

It was not this way when the world was first created, when "God saw everything that He had made, and indeed it was very good" (Genesis 1:31 NKJV). The present reality, however, gives evidence that we live in a corrupted, fallen world. There are two reasons for this. First, humankind's disobedience brought a curse upon the earth (Genesis 3:17–18; Isaiah 24:5–6). This was likely when existing, beneficial bacteria and viruses mutated and became malignant.

Also, UV radiation from the sun is a leading cause of damage to DNA, and scientists state that the earth's magnetic field, which (together with the ozone layer) protects us from UV rays, was three times stronger during the days of the dinosaurs. Many Christians also believe that a shield of ice crystals once surrounded the earth. When this shield fell as rain (Genesis 7:11–12), or the other shields were weakened, the damage in our DNA began to accumulate.

> **ArchaeoLogic:** Pharaoh Merneptah (1213–1203 BC) invaded Canaan, and his victory stele, discovered in 1896, contains the earliest extra-biblical mention of Israel, saying, among other things: "Canaan has been plundered. . . . Israel is laid waste and his seed is not."

73. God Loves and Cares

The previous answers may make God sound like the absentee watchmaker who created the world and its inhabitants, then left us alone—but God isn't absent. He's aware of what's happening in all Creation (Luke 12:6–7). But it is true that having set the earth in motion around the sun, He doesn't have to constantly reinvent the laws of physics to keep it moving.

In the same way, He's also active in our lives, but doesn't interfere with our free will. Paul said, "In the past he permitted all the nations to go their own ways, but he never left them without evidence of himself and his goodness" (Acts 14:16–17 NLT). God showed His love to all people, but He chose one nation to which He directly manifested His presence and His power. He told Israel, "I am making a covenant with you. Before all your people I will do wonders never before done in any nation in all the world" (Exodus 34:10 NIV). He was even actively involved with the weather of their land (Deuteronomy 11:11–12 NKJV).

God then proved His great love and care for humanity (not just for the Israelites, but for all nations) by personally entering our fallen, corrupted world: He sent his Son, Jesus Christ, who healed the sick and spoke up for the oppressed and poor; Jesus experienced all the temptations that we do, and ultimately suffered and died for our sakes, to give us new life. He not only taught us and showed us how to live but also promised to send His Spirit into our hearts to give us the power to live this life.

74. God Is Active in the World

You may feel that God is distant and doesn't care about the sufferings of this world, but He has great compassion and has set a plan in motion to tangibly meet people's needs. When you read the New Testament slowly and carefully, you get the clear message that God wants Christians—who have the Spirit of Jesus living in them—to be His boots on the ground, His hands of mercy to the suffering.

We are to be actively involved in feeding the hungry, clothing the poor, speaking out for the oppressed, and giving financially to help disaster victims. Read Matthew 25:31–46, and you'll see what it means to be a follower of Jesus Christ. Read Luke 10:25–37, and you'll understand God's compassion for the world and His plan to relieve its suffering. This passage also shows that all people deserve our help, regardless of their race, culture, or religion.

When the early Christians learned that a worldwide famine would hit Judea hard, "the disciples, each according to his ability, determined to send relief to the brethren dwelling in Judea" (Acts 11:29 NKJV). "If anyone has material possessions and sees a brother or sister in need but has no pity on them, how can the love of God be in that person? Dear children, let us not love with words or speech but with actions and in truth" (1 John 3:17–18 NIV).

This is why Christians, down through the ages

until the present day, have been leaders in doing acts of mercy and compassion—they feed the poor, build orphanages and hospitals, care for lepers, staff homeless shelters and soup kitchens, and fund relief organizations.

> **ArchaeoLogic:** Paul's enemies in Corinth dragged him before Governor Gallio's judgment seat (bema) to be judged, but Gallio dismissed the case (Acts 18:12–17). This very bema has been excavated. It is a large stone edifice rising 7.5 feet above the side of the public market.

75. We Shall Understand Someday

"Come now, and let us reason together, saith the LORD" (Isaiah 1:18 KJV). If you have questions, know that the Bible contains answers. God invites you to read His Word, to try to reason things out, and to pray for Him to help you understand. But many things, especially details of why painful things have happened in your life, are not easy to figure out.

And bear in mind that, comparatively speaking, we're working with grade school addition, wondering why things don't add up, while God is working with advanced mathematical formulas. Many things we're not aware of must be factored into the equation. "'For My thoughts are not your thoughts, nor are your ways My ways,' says the LORD. 'For as the heavens are higher than the earth, so are My ways higher than your ways, and My thoughts than your thoughts'" (Isaiah 55:8–9 NKJV).

We won't be able to understand the answers to some difficult questions, such as why suffering occurred, until we go to heaven and enter the presence of God. "Now we see things imperfectly. . .but then we will see everything with perfect clarity. All that I know now is partial and incomplete, but then I will know everything completely" (1 Corinthians 13:12 NLT).

Not only God will also explain things that we weren't able to understand before, but also all suffering will come to an end. "And God will wipe away every tear from their eyes; there shall be no more death, nor sorrow, nor crying. There shall be no more pain, for the former things have passed away" (Revelation 21:4 NKJV).

If you enjoyed

WHY THE BIBLE MAKES SENSE

be sure to look for these other great Bible
resources from Barbour Publishing!

The Complete Guide to the Bible
Paperback, 528 pages
ISBN 978-1-59789-374-9

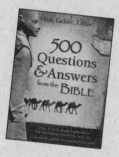

500 Questions & Answers
from the Bible
Paperback, 256 pages
ISBN 978-1-59789-473-9

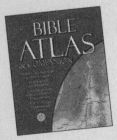

Bible Atlas & Companion
Paperback, 176 pages
ISBN 978-1-59789-779-2

Available wherever Christian books are sold.